An incident at the Battle of Firket during the
Dongola Campaign: Captain Fitton's horse is
shot under him.

KHAKI & RED

SOLDIERS OF THE QUEEN IN INDIA AND AFRICA
Donald Featherstone

Left: Slatin Pasha, one of the many colourful figures of the Sudan campaigns, stands in contemplation of the body of his friend and enemy, the Emir Hammuda, general of the Mahdi's army, dead on the battlefield.

ARMS AND
ARMOUR

Arms and Armour Press
An Imprint of the Cassell Group
Wellington House, 125 Strand,
London WC2R 0BB

Distributed in the USA by Sterling Publishing
Co. Inc., 387 Park Avenue South, New York,
NY 10016-8810

First published 1995
This paperback edition 1997

British Library Cataloguing-in-Publication
Data: a catalogue record for this book is
available from the British Library

ISBN 1-85409-425-4

Designed and edited by DAG Publications
Ltd. Designed by David Gibbons; layout by
Anthony A. Evans; edited by Michael Boxall;
printed and bound in Great Britain.

Publisher's Note
The illustrations in this book have been
gathered from a variety of nineteenth-
century sources, and some may be deemed
to fall short of the standards of reproduction
to be expected in a modern book. They are
nevertheless included here for their intrinsic
information value, many having been prepared by artists in the field.

Jacket illustration:
*The Charge of the
21st Lancers at
Omdurman* by
George Delville
Rowlandson, 1898.
Reproduced by
courtesy of the
17th/21st Lancers'
Museum, Belvoir
Castle.

OTHER PUBLISHED TITLES BY DON FEATHERSTONE

All for a Shilling a Day
MacDonald of the 42nd
Captain Carey's Blunder
At them With the Bayonet!
Colonial Small Wars, 1837–1901
Conflict in Hampshire
The Bowmen of England
Weapons & Equipment of the Victorian Soldier
Victoria's Enemies – 19th Century Colonial Wars
Khartoum; the Gordon Relief Expedition, 1884–5
Tel-el-Kebir; the War with Egypt 1882
Omdurman; Kitchener's Dongola Campaign, 1896-8
Victorian Military Campaigns in Africa
Victorian Military Campaigns in India
*Campaigning With the Duke of Wellington
and Featherstone; Peninsular War, 1808–14*
Featherstone's Complete Wargaming
Wargames
Naval Wargames
Air Wargames
Advanced Wargames
Wargames Campaigns

Battles With Model Soldiers
*Wargames Through The Ages: vol.1 3000 BC – AD
1500; vol. 2 1420–1783; vol. 3 1792–1859; vol. 4
1861–1945*
Poitiers 1356 – Battle For Wargames
Battle Notes For Wargamers
Solo Wargaming
*Tank Battles In Miniature: The Western Desert
Campaign*
Tank Battles In Miniature: The Mediterranean Theatre
Skirmish Wargames
Wargaming The Ancient And Medieval Periods
Wargaming The Pike And Shot Period
*The Wargamer's Handbook Of The American
Revolution*
Wargaming Airborne Operations
Battles With Model Tanks (With Keith Robinson)
Tackle Model Soldiers This Way
Handbook For Model Soldier Collectors
Military Modelling
Better Military Modelling
Wargaming In History – The Peninsular War

Contents

Prologue

Throughout the Victorian Era, for sixty-four years, in red coats or dusty khaki, men from every British shire and county marched alongside their native allies in slow-moving columns, elephants jostling camels and bullocks plodding with donkeys and yaks, to a background jingle of mule-carried mountain guns. Sometimes, parties of boisterous straw-hatted sailors and Royal Marines, led by such dashing officers as Lord Charles Beresford, dragged Gatling and Gardner guns through the sand of the Sudan where, treating camels like leaking boats, they caulked their huge sores with pitch. Typical yet unique, each campaign was made notable by the men who fought them – the Regular British soldier, grumbling but obeying orders and doing his duty against militant tribesmen on the rugged North-West Frontier of India; subduing stubborn Boers, brave Maoris, wily Afghans, or fierce and fanatical Dervishes; battling against organised military formations of Sikhs, Zulus, Russians or rebellious India Sepoys. None of this great variety of opponents fought in the same fashion and rarely was there any prior knowledge of their strength, weapons, fighting ability, or methods of warfare – yet all were eventually beaten.

PART ONE
THE VICTORIAN MILITARY SCENE

The Battle of Firket, during the Dongola Campaign.

1
Wars in Which British Soldiers Fought, 1837–1900

Queen Victoria came to the throne of Great Britain on 20 June 1837, during a rare period when British soldiers were not fighting on foreign soil; within three months, however, Sir John Colborne's force was busily quelling rebellious Canadians. During the sixty-four years that followed, the Queen's name signified an era when the wide spread of British rule brought Western-style civilisation to an increasingly growing Empire. Chauvinism and nostalgia lend credence to the belief that it was a great and glorious period of British history, when hardly a year passed without the Army being engaged in some far-flung corner of the five Continents, fighting more than four hundred pitched battles in more than sixty campaigns. Occasionally the emotions of the British public were aroused by news of a hard-pressed garrison being relieved, otherwise there was precious little stimulation in the bare details of small-scale and hard-fought affrays against fierce native foes, harsh tropical climates and virulent disease. Casualties were often relatively light because the soldier was better armed and disciplined, but when up against a natural warrior on his own terrain and unafraid of death, losses could be unpleasantly heavy.

During this sixty-four-year period, the British soldier encountered many diverse foes of innumerable nations, countries, tribes and sects. Among them were Abyssinians; Afghans; Afridis; Arabs; Ashantis; Australians; Baluchis; Bengalis; Boers; Bunerwals; Burmese; Canadians; Chamlawals; Chamkannis; Chinese; Chitralis; Dervishes; Egyptians; Fingoes; Gaikas; Galekas; Ghazis; Hadendowahs; Hassanzais; Hottentots; Hunzas; Indians; Isazais; Japanese; Jowaki Afridis; Kaffirs; Khudu-Khels; Kodakhel Baezais; Kostwals; Lushais; Madda Khels; Mahrattas; Mahsud Wazirs; Malays; Mangals; Maoris; Mashonas; Masais; Matabeles; Mohmands; Orakzais; Pathans; Peraks; Persians; Punjabis; Russians; Sepoys; Shinwaris; Shiranis; Sikhs; Somalis; Sudanese; Tibetans; Utman Khels; Wazaris; Zaimukhts; Zakha Khel Afridis, and Zulus.

The wars and campaigns in which this multiplicity of foes were encountered, anomalously in an era marked by victorious conflicts against native opponents, began and ended with the subduing of white opponents – rebellious Canadians in 1837 and, at the time of the old Queen's death on 22 January 1901, the Boer leader De Wet who was concentrating his forces for a fresh invasion of Cape Colony.

Victorian 'Small' Wars, expeditions and campaigns undertaken by the Queen's disciplined soldiers and their native allies, frequently developed into campaigns of conquest or the annexation of vast countries and territories to the British Crown. These campaigns might be mounted to suppress rebellion or lawlessness in annexed territories, or to avenge a wrong, wipe out an insult by sending a punitive force to chastise or overthrow a dangerous or troublesome enemy, or might be wars of expediency fought for political reasons, such as that in Egypt in 1882. Primitive conditions and the enemy's peculiar style of fighting meant that these wars diverged widely from the conditions and principles of regular warfare, when each side was well aware of what to expect from the enemy, both being governed by common rules. It was an era during which all manner of opponents were encountered, with little prior knowledge of their strength, weapons, fighting abilities or methods of warfare – the only constant being that all of them fought differently. For example, although organised on the Zulu system, the Matabele did not possess such a high degree of efficiency and, not being such great natural warriors, were nowhere near as formidable as the Zulu *impis*. The Sudanese and the Afghan Ghazi lacked Zulu discipline, but fought with a bravery and recklessness that necessitated a return to outmoded tactics of tight battle-formations. Other opponents such as the Chinese, the Ashantis, and the hillmen of the North-West Frontier of India fought in a totally different fashion, but all usually managed to put up a very stern resistance. Each presented new and unusual features which, if not foreseen, brought difficulty and sometimes grievous misfortune to the Regular troops.

The terrain over which the fighting took place played a major part. For example, the Kaffirs in South Africa, were not particularly noted for courage and were poorly armed, but the manner in which they utilised the natural and familiar features of their bush and jungle made them difficult to subdue.

There were few barren years. Always in season, Victorian Colonial Wars regularly and remorselessly broke out in the most diverse corners of the world. Thus:

1837	Canada
1838	Aden — Afghanistan
1840	China — The Levant
1841	Afghanistan — China
1842	Afghanistan
1843	Gwalior — Sind
1845	The Punjab — South Africa
1846	The Punjab — South Africa
1847	South Africa
1848	NW Frontier — Punjab — South Africa
1849	NW Frontier — Punjab — South Africa
1850	NW Frontier
1851	South Africa
1852	Burma — NW Frontier — South Africa
1853	NW Frontier
1854	Australia — NW Frontier — Crimea (Russia)
1855	Crimea
1856	Crimea — Persia
1857	Oudh and Bengal — Persia

1858	Oudh and Bengal — Central India
1859	Oudh and Bengal — China
1860	China
1861	New Zealand — Sikkim (India)
1862	New Zealand
1863	New Zealand — Ambela (NW Frontier)
1864	New Zealand — Bhutan — Japan — NW Frontier
1865	Bhutan
1866–7	NW Frontier
1868	Abyssinia
1870	Canada
1871	Lushai (India)
1874	Ashanti
1875	Perak (Malay)
1876	Perak (Malay)
1877	NW Frontier — South Africa
1878	Afghanistan — NW Frontier — Malta
1879	Afghanistan — NW Frontier — Natal — South Africa — Zululand
1880	NW Frontier
1881	NW Frontier — Transvaal (South Africa)
1882	Egypt
1884	Burma — NW Frontier — Sudan
1885	Burma — Sudan
1888	NW Frontier — Sikkim (India) — Tibet
1890	NW Frontier — Somaliland
1891	NW Frontier — Hunza (India) — Manipur (India) — Burma
1892	NW Frontier — Chilas (India)
1894	Waziristan (India)
1895	Chitral (India)
1896	Mashonaland — Egypt — Mombasa — Zanzibar
1897	Benin — Tirah — Egypt (Sudan) — NW Frontier (Malakand / Tochi)
1898	Buner (India) — Juberland — Niger — South Africa (Transvaal)
1899	South Africa (Transvaal)
1900	South Africa (Transvaal) — Ashanti — China
1901	South Africa (Transvaal) — China

Throughout these years, apart from Canadian Fenians and South African Boers, the only white-faced opponents to confront the British Regular Army were Russians in the Crimea in 1854–6 and, in the same year, rebellious Australian gold-miners.

The years 1879 and 1880 were marked by two of the greatest military disasters of the Victorian era, when Cetewayo's Zulus wiped out a British force at Isandhlwana, and an Afghan army of about 12,000 men defeated Burroughs' Anglo-Indian force of 2,300 at Maiwand. In mitigation, it should be mentioned that this was in the middle of a three-year period when, in a single quarter of the African continent, British troops came successively into conflict with the extremely diverse methods of fighting of Kaffirs, Zulus and Boers, while at the same time being heavily committed on the North-West Frontier of India and Afghanistan.

The problems of guerrilla warfare were endemic when campaigning on the North-West Frontier of India, where

11

well-armed and fanatical tribesmen took full advantage of a severe and harsh terrain well suited to their style of fighting. This was not invariably the case and some enemies did not utilise familiar terrain or fight in their accustomed style, as with the Ashantis who never flinched from risking a general and open engagement if they felt it would bring them victory.

On many occasions sickness caused greater losses than did battle and more often than not campaigns degenerated into struggles against Nature rather than hostile armies. Unaccustomed climatic conditions grievously affected the health of the Regular troops, while lack of communications prevented evacuation of sick and wounded, besides limiting supplies. In most of these 'small' wars Regular forces were at an undoubted strategical disadvantage, despite the backing of the resources of state-of-the-art science, wealth, manpower, and navies. The strength of these factors actually represented virtual weakness, because the arms and equipment required to ensure tactical superiority and eventual success, required long non-combat 'tails' tied to bases and lines of communication.

Not all the enemy encountered in Victorian Colonial Wars were savage or irregular warriors; some wars were fought against an enemy trained and organised as regular troops by instructors with knowledge and experience of European methods, so that subsequent operations resembled the conventional warfare of the time. It occurred in the Punjab in 1845–6 and in 1849 when, after some of the fiercest fighting in British Colonial history, the British regiments of the East India Company – inauspiciously supported by native troops – defeated the martial Sikhs. The 1857 Mutiny in India found British Regulars and loyal native units faced by field armies in superior numbers, composed of experienced and competent Sepoys trained along British lines. In the Crimea the British and their French allies were opposed by a trained and well-armed European army which, had it not been commanded in an even more inefficient manner than that of the Allies, could have resulted, in that harsh climate, in a major disaster. In 1882, Arabi Pasha led a well-armed, trained and disciplined Egyptian Army to defeat by Wolseley at Kassassin and Tel-el-Kebir, while two years earlier, a trained Regular Afghan army, with Russian-trained artillery officers, defeated Burroughs' smaller Anglo-Indian force at Maiwand.

What has been written so far could well be criticised as a saga of pacification and punishment in four continents, and held up as rabid anti-colonial propaganda. But when considering colonialism it should be remembered that in the 19th century the British successfully organised and maintained military and police formations from the people of regions recently conquered in Africa, India, Asia, Borneo, and the West Indies – and in every case it worked with harmony and loyalty. Entering their country as an invader, the British soldier invariably became a respected friend through his innate gift of making himself intelligible to all peoples, nations and languages. In truth it was an age when, as a matter of routine, small forces under energetic commanders pacified frontiers, quelled rebellions and administered vast tracts of territory. Queen Victoria, deeply conscious of her position as Queen-Empress, held high-minded concepts of Empire and a faith in Britain's Imperial destiny that was shared by that remarkable assortment of strong-minded generals who, throughout her reign, were blessed with the ability and fortune almost invariably to be in the right place at the right time.

2

The Victorian Army

The Victorian period saw immense changes and advances in almost every aspect of life, yet the British Army altered so little that the line infantryman who fought at Waterloo in 1815 would have found few tactical problems in taking his place in the ranks at Omdurman in 1898. Until the 1850s, lacking the stimulation of a Waterloo, the Army refused to accept changes other than those that stemmed from the glorious traditions of the past. In this they were unremittingly directed by the Duke of Wellington, Britain's supreme and unchallengeable military authority, whose stern dictates so long shackled the British Army to the methods of the Napoleonic Wars of half-a-century earlier. Steadfastly supported by a succession of Adjutants-General and backed by Parliament, the Duke dismissed the progressive advance of military science in Continental nations by quoting his inflexible maxim that what had been accomplished before could be achieved again with the same instruments. His victories with the old smoothbore Brown Bess convinced him that artillery was an inferior weapon to the musket, the soldier fought best when encumbered with heavy accoutrements, uncomfortable chokers, suffocating stocks and restricting ill-slung knapsacks. The Duke believed that the nation would resent the Army if it became too costly, so he doggedly opposed increases in pay and kept his soldiers out of sight in overcrowded back-street barracks. In this he was supported by a succession of governments convinced that more money would make the soldier increasingly licentious and drunken and so necessitate greater severity and discipline.

The old Duke died in 1854, just before the Crimean War, which was fought by hardened soldiers of the Old School – illiterate, foul-mouthed, solid, shrewd and long-suffering, prematurely-aged by harsh barrack conditions at home and gruelling colonial campaigns overseas – and drunkenness. It took the unremitting efforts of two outstanding reforming-spirits, Secretary-at-War Sydney Herbert and Florence Nightingale, to change the old order and introduce a milder atmosphere into the life of the Army, as the long-service soldier died in the Crimea or faded from the scene, taking with him many of the bad old ideas.

The Chobham Camp of Exercise in 1853 and the development of Aldershot Camp provided regiments and soldiers with outdoor training facilities. But past wars had been won without such preparation that interfered with farming and the grazing-rights of common land. At this time the Army of the Honourable East India Company conducted their colonial wars in a far more practical manner than did the Home Army, yet its successes were not allowed in any way to affect the moribund methods that passed for training in Britain. Fortuitously, when the Indian Mutiny saw the end of the Company's Army, an obliging militant, mobile and tactically efficient native enemy on the North-West Frontier of India provided a most effective battle training ground that was to benefit the British soldier for the next 90 years.

During the Crimean War the public were shocked into changing their attitudes towards their soldiers by newspaper reports and letters via the new Army Post telling of their appalling suffering at Sevastopol and in the hospital at Scutari, where Florence Nightingale and her nurses soon learned that the British soldier was a simple person who reacted favourably to gentle treatment.

Rejecting early attempts to blame the soldiers for Crimean blunders, the British public, acknowledging that much of the fault was theirs, began to reveal an irrational inarticulate admiration for their soldiers and, without ostentatiously mending their ways, saved face by treating returning men as heroes. The national conscience was aroused and past neglect remedied by including the soldier and his family in the extensive humanising of the daily life of the people that was in full swing. Acknowledging that military life was far removed from the familiar workaday world of the time, writers and journalists sought new qualities in the soldiers. Thus, in a prelude to *The Great Tasmania* Charles Dickens wrote inspiringly of the British soldier:-

'Any animated description of a modern battle, any private soldier's letter published in the newspapers, any page of the records of the Victoria Cross will show in the ranks of the army there exists under all disadvantage as fine a sense of duty as is to be found in any

station on earth. Who doubts that if we all did our duty as faithfully as a soldier does his, this world would be a better place? There may be greater difficulties in our way than in the soldiers. Not disputed. But let us at least do our duty towards *him*.'

It was recalled how Dr Johnson, who had a shrewd insight into what made the world go round, had spoken of the military:-

'The qualities which make any army formidable are long habits of regularity, great exactness of discipline and great confidence in the commander.' He gave as his opinion that '... discipline was often indifferent and that they had no particular reasons to be confident in their commanders; yet they were without doubt the bravest soldiers in the world.'

Repeated scares of French invasion during the second half of the 19th century together with improved communications that allowed extensive coverage of colonial wars produced a marked improvement in the attitude of

Left: British Line Infantry, 1846.

the British public towards their soldiers – they might not have any greater understanding of military affairs nor did it result in any substantial improvement in recruiting but it did set the fashion for Tommy Atkins to be regarded as a sort of domestic pet. The Diamond Jubilee of 1897 aroused affection and respect for the aged Queen whose known regard for her soldiers, particularly the Highland regiments, produced a wave of sentimental feeling for the Army. The Boer War turned the British people into a nation of patriots who fêted soldiers as heroes and rushed to shake hands with them while they sang 'Goodbye Dolly Gray'. As the 19th century drew slowly to its end, together with the life of the Queen who had given her name to an era, the British public revelled in an unshakable belief that their soldiers were more than a match for any foreigners, expressing their sentiments forcibly:

'And when we say we always won,
And when they ask us how its done,
We proudly point to every one
Of the soldiers of the Queen.'

Unshaken by the disasters of the Boer War, this jingoistic conviction was built on firm foundations as the man in the ranks, still a Victorian soldier for a few more months, fought and died bravely against the Boers as he had always done against Sikh and Zulu, Pathan and Dervish. On those few occasions when he had not come out on top, it was usually the fault of those who led him, and on numerous occasions he had redeemed brave errors of leadership by conduct well beyond what might have been expected of him. Rarely did he fail ignominiously, although there were occasions during both First and Second Boer Wars when the public were shocked to read of un-British lapses and attitudes – mostly due to military mis-management and

defects in commanders. It is surprising that there should have been so few of these episodes considering that for most of the Victorian period the Army was formed of the dregs of the nation transformed in relatively short time, by training and discipline, from an armed rabble into a fine instrument of war.

As the century ran its course, the British soldier found himself spending less and less time in Britain. His entitlement to five years at home for every ten years spent overseas could only be fulfilled by steadily reducing overseas garrisons, so that any threatening situation in India or Africa cut into already curtailed periods of home service. To these lengthy periods overseas were added the months spent at sea on passage to and from remote parts of the Empire when, in those early days of steam, both the perils of the sea and generally atrocious conditions had to be endured aboard troopships. But even this was preferable to the stifling routine and initiative-suppressing slow-poison of Home Service that could drug even the ambitious, strong-minded officer or man into a state of inertia. But if the British soldier lacked the intellect and background to fight off such a reaction, his burning desire for Active Service enabled him to retain his undoubted character and constitutional courage so that when called upon he could fight, and sometimes die, as bravely and notably as did his ancestors, and often on the same foreign fields.

In the earlier part of the Victorian era a girl who married a soldier let herself in for a hard life, cutting herself off from her family and from what passed as 'decent society', following her man through the hardships of tropical heat, cold, dysentery, cholera, malaria; bearing and rearing children in barrack rooms, fighting with other wives when drunk, nursing the sick, writing letters, washing and sewing as she played her

rough, often coarse part in the Army of her day. In peacetime she went overseas with her husband's regiment, otherwise she was abandoned at home – there were no Marriage Allowances. There were no recognised married quarters abroad so families were accommodated in return for wives performing various domestic duties for her husband's comrades and, without any training, nursing the sick and wounded. From the Restoration until the Crimean War it was the custom for six wives per company (or 100 men) to be drawn by lot to accompany their husbands overseas on Active Service. Fear of being left behind was a perpetual nightmare, sometimes wives and children straggled for days behind the regiment to be left crying on the jetty as the husband she would probably never see again peered distraughtly from the throng of faces aboard the troopship. Those who went with their husbands must have been a very tough breed to withstand the harsh living conditions on campaign. Some of the most touching and human stories of the British soldier must revolve around women brave enough to marry a soldier and bear his children. By the late 19th century, the lot of the soldier's wife and children had improved so that a reasonable domestic existence was possible in Married Quarters or when 'Living Out'.

Before the Cardwell Reforms, soldiers engaged to serve for up to 21 years, and a soldier 'belonged' to his commanding officer whose whim decided whether he was permitted to live in the married state. The Queen had reigned for 20 years before any attempt was made to provide separate accommodation for married soldiers; before that he, his wife and children all lived in a corner of the barrack room screened off with grubby tattered blankets; the creak of a bed could arouse ribald laughter and vulgarity from his mates in the overcrowded room. In 1855 at Aldershot, one hut or room was reserved in each regimental block for eight or ten married soldiers and their families, blankets or wet-washing screens around the beds provided sparse privacy, cooking was carried out on a communal stove or fire in the centre of the room. In the 1870s a married recruit had no 'indulgence' and his wife, being 'unrecognised', could not live in barracks or draw rations of bread, meat and coal like the wives of those soldiers married with the Colonel's permission, after serving seven years. In 1865, although married quarters had been erected, most families were still living in communal barrack rooms with inadequate sanitary facilities.

The Cardwell Reforms produced the new Short Service soldier who did not require consideration as a married man in barracks, thus it was possible to house smaller numbers to improved standards. As time passed, it was only relatively senior soldiers and re-engaging private soldiers for whom married quarters were required. But a private was only allocated quarters 'if avail-

able', so only a limited number of married privates could be carried on the strength of the regiment, i.e., receive official permission to marry – which had to be obtained at the same time as his claim for married-quarters was considered. It rested with the commanding officer whether a soldier, his wife and children lived in comparative comfort in quarters, or existed outside the regiment without financial aid other than that earned by the wife. Men *did* marry 'off the strength', to live on a shilling a day, plus the man's rations, with the wife doing laundry work or sewing to make extra money.

The reforms instituted in 1870–82 by Lord Edward Cardwell, Secretary of State for War, though their implementation was as slow and ponderous as the Victorian age that produced them, brought revolutionary changes to produce a 'new' army. The 'old soldier', no longer over 40 (looking 60), was a young man in the prime of life with superior habits of cleanliness, reasonable sobriety and discipline compared with his civilian counterpart, attracted into the army by the new short-service enlistments. This brought about a gradual diminishment in the chronic civilian aversion towards anything military, and old prejudices against soldiers began to fade.

From beginning to end of the Victorian era the Army, unactuated by any profound motives of patriotism or thought for great national causes, doggedly pursued its programme of small colonial campaigns and overseas expeditions that were insignificant far-distant affairs, often punitive at first but culminating in vast territorial acquisitions. On occasions the means and the ends might have seemed inglorious, but invariably the soldiers themselves innately revealed qualities that produced performances far better than could reasonably have been expected of them.

3
The Victorian Soldier

Perhaps the most remarkable feature of the many 'small' wars of Queen Victoria's reign were the men who fought them for her, shown on strength returns not as individuals, but as so many 'rifles' or 'sabres', taken over by another man in the event of the original owner being killed or wounded. So, it might be asked – 'Who were they?', these uncouth hearty men who occasionally erupted from their disciplined seclusion into fusty police-courts, to be tagged as drunken and diseased reprobates. Or, to burst upon public consciousness as the heroes of romantic and courageous episodes in far-distant corners of the Empire – as the 'Thin Red Line' at Balaclava, the storming-columns at Delhi, the gallant defenders of Rorke's Drift, or the relievers of Mafeking.

The romantic nature of the late Victorian period thrived on the quite unrealistic paintings of military heroism produced by Lady Butler, Caton Woodville and others, backed by the stirring woodcut prints drawn by military artists on far-flung battlefields and reproduced in *Illustrated London News* and *The Graphic*. The public began to be inspired by the bearing and courage of the soldiers representing them in India, Africa and the Sudan, particularly when brave deeds were done by a regiment from a specific locality – all Berkshire went into mourning when their County regiment was wiped out at Maiwand in 1880. At Isandhlwana in 1879, an army of Zulus massacred most of the 24th Foot (the South Wales Borderers) leaving a single company that won seven VCs on the following day at Rorke's Drift – it was well within the spirit of the time for Queen Victoria to place a wreath of immortelles on the regimental Queen's Colour.

Until the middle of the century, the British Army consisted of prematurely aged, hardened soldiers of the old school, stolid, shrewd, long-suffering coarse blasphemous men who nurtured a thirst that needed constant slaking. Early Victorian soldiers wore beards, in the 1870s they had to shave them off, being given the choice of wearing whiskers with a moustache or a moustache alone; their hair was cropped close to the head by company or regimental barbers. Many of them had elaborate designs tattooed on their arms and body, the best known being a pack of hounds running down the man's back in full-cry after a fox whose tail was disappearing into the man's rectum.

Swearing coldly from between clenched teeth, they habitually used bad language and dotted their conversations with Hindustani and Arabic expressions so that bread was always

Right: An officer of the Grenadier Guards photographed before leaving for Egypt, 1882.

'roti', water 'pani' and beer 'pongelow'; food was 'skof' and the cook the 'bobbajee'; to be under arrest was to be 'on the peg' and prison was 'college'. Work was 'graft' and the 'grouser' groused about it; arguing made him a 'barrack room lawyer' or he might be a 'Queen's bad bargain' who, turning over a new leaf, was said to be 'on the cot'. The recruit was a 'rooky', the veteran 'an old sweat' and the soldier always spoke of himself as a 'swaddy'; his lady-friend was a 'pusher' with whom he 'square-pushed'; the teetotaller was a 'bun strangler' or 'pop-wallah'. His bed his 'kip', his helmet his 'topee' and uniform 'clobber', working-clothes were 'fatigues'; boots were 'daisy-roots' (later 'ammunitions') and his customary meal of bread and coffee was always known as 'slingers'.

This exclusive dialect, together with a host of harsh customs and traditions, enslaved both mind and body so that civilian days became an unreal nostalgic recollection inevitably leading to a rosy and artificial vision of life when soldiering was done. He never envied civilians their peace, comfort and freedom from danger – in return they treated him with distaste, contempt and neglect, completely failing to recognise that his vices were no worse or more frequent than those they displayed themselves in an era of habitual brutality and hard-living, starvation wages and repressive work-conditions, with barbaric public exhibitions of punishments. Grudgingly acknowledging them as lions in war, the public saw the soldiers as wolves in peacetime, forgetting the extenuating circumstances of their miserable life-condition – choked in tight leather stocks, cheated of pay, flogged for a trifle and shipped abroad like cattle in filthy troopships.

For much of the 19th century, the almost total absence of organised social amenities and recreational facilities, combined with lack of education that might stimulate the soldier to seek them, caused him inevitably to turn to drink as a cheap and convenient means of temporarily forgetting the misery and squalor of his monotonous, bullied existence. Overseas the one common factor of all foreign stations was cheap liquor, whether it brought profit to the Government by being sold in the canteens, or native-brewed using wood-alcohol that could cause blindness or painful death. Their lives of habitual repression prevented many soldiers from becoming genially drunk; rather they became consumed with a smouldering hate and anger that made them over-sensitive to fancied slights and insults so that each cobbled street had its reeling party of drunken soldiers in black and ugly mood, spoiling for a fight.

Dangerous traditional antipathies arising from some obscure grievance of half a century earlier were well-known to exist between regiments, surviving as ancient feuds that shook garrison-towns to their very foundations when grim purposeful mauls were fought out with fists, belts, bottles, sticks, stones, and sometimes bayonets. Invariably such fracas occurred on pay-nights because only then did the soldier have money to buy sufficient drink to make him quarrelsome; in time a system of staggered pay-days ensured that neighbouring units did not get drunk on the same night. After allowing the men to fight long enough to 'work off steam', patrols wielding pickaxe handles doubled out of barracks and broke-up the struggling mobs; sober and irritated at having their rest disturbed, the patrols laid about them vigorously and the men they dragged back to the cells, sometimes in hand-cuffs, were much the worse for wear.

Almost to the end of the Victorian era the British public moulded the soldier into all they considered him to be – an un-thinking, blindly-disciplined unintelligent man of doubtful morality, to be treated and ridiculed as an outcast. The British man-in-the-ranks was reputed to be '... full of beer, beef and lust', notorious for his violent and evil way of life; apparently stupid and stolid, reacting only to shouting and swearing, he was despised more by the British public than the equally rough and hard-drinking navvy whose wild and undisciplined life-style aroused a grudging respect. In this age of hard living and harsh punishment, the soldier's vices were plainly no worse than those displayed in civilian life, yet he was summarily consigned to a limbo without any compensation for the discomforts and general misery of his condition in a calling that put life and limb at risk. The generally accepted view of the redcoat as the scum of the earth, beyond the bounds of civilised society, meant that many publicans would not admit into their

Below: British Cavalry in Egypt, 1882. (Orlando Norie Watercolour.)

bar a man wearing the Queen's uniform, and he was usually turned away at the door of theatre or music-hall. Inevitably such ostracism moulded the soldier into a social misfit with a drab life that encouraged excessive drinking and with his physical needs assuaged by sordid sexual adventures, often ending in venereal diseases.

The respectable working class regarded 'going for a soldier' to be synonymous with going to the bad and a final degradation – the simple-minded self-respecting rustic was ashamed to admit to having a son in the army. The London tradesman, northern farmer and Scottish crofter were united in their belief that the army was a den of lawless, licentious cut-throats and drunken thieves and would ruthlessly cut-off any daughter who committed the heinous crime of marrying a serving soldier. Prim mistresses, horrified at the thought of even second- or third-hand contact with those 'awful men who were filled with beef, beer and lust', dismissed without notice parlour-maids and below-stairs female servants seen in company with a red-coat. The soldier also received the harshest treatment from his immediate superiors although, wearing the same uniform, they were marked as members of a solitary caste of untouchables unhealthily living under appalling conditions in insanitary barracks.

The derisive tone habitually employed when writing of the soldier was reflected by Michael Titmarsh in *Punch*:

'The whole system of the army is something egregious and artificial. The civilian who lives out of it cannot understand it. It is not like other professions which require intelligence. The man one degree removed from idiocy, with brains sufficient to direct his powers of mischief and endurance, may make a distinguished soldier. As to the men, they get the word of command to advance or to fall back, and they do it; they are told to strip and be flogged and they do it, or to flog and they do it; to murder or be murdered, and they obey; for their food and clothing and two pence a day for their tobacco.'

Lacking schooling, it was not surprising that most soldiers were illiterate, which prevented the tedium of his life to be relieved by reading. Even so, in the first half of the 19th century, the only books allowed in barracks were those on a prescribed list of 28 volumes that had been approved by a bench of bishops, intent on preventing subversive literature reaching the man-in-the-ranks.

Not many soldiers read books or newspapers – in fact, 60 per cent of the soldiers of Crimean War Line Infantry regiments were illiterate. Mainly through fear of making him vulnerable to revolutionary propaganda, there was very little attempt to educate the soldier during the Duke of Wellington's years of influence. In the late 1840s Sydney Herbert began educational reforms despite the marked distaste of the average soldier for any imposed form of book-learning. In 1860 at Sevastopol, Sergeant T. Gowing (7th Royal Fusiliers) was beset by his comrades to write letters home and penned more than twenty short notes. In the early 1870s Troop Sergeant-Major E. Mole of the 14th Hussars was the only man out of fifteen in his barrack room who could read and write so that he was in great demand to read letters for his comrades and to write answers to them. In return, they cleaned and polished his arms and accoutrements.

Literacy bestowed upon the soldier a certain social status in the barrack room just as the possession of a watch was regarded as a badge of character and the man so endowed was reputedly careful of his belongings, saved his pay and spent little on drink – he was also nicknamed 'Ticker'. If the watch-owner was slovenly his time-piece would quickly be broken or stolen, if a drunkard it would soon be pawned to buy beer. Not one soldier in five hundred had a watch and few bought them during the course of military life; if parents or sweetheart gave him a watch as a present it was extremely likely that he would be parted from it within a year. In 1877, when No.1514 Trooper William Robertson (later to become the first man to rise from the ranks to become a field marshal) was posted to 'G' Troop of the 16th Lancers, his officer advised him: 'Give your watch to the sergeant-major, for it is unsafe to leave it lying about and there is nowhere you can carry it with safety.'

Men 'took on for soldiers' through stark necessity – the potato famines drove young Irishmen into the British Army as the only means of obtaining food, clothing and a roof over their heads. For much of the mid-19th century regimental rolls resembled Irish parish registers and the inexorable march of the British Empire was milestoned by graves bearing Irish names. As it had been for centuries, the Army was still an asylum for the scourings of the nation with magistrates giving prisoners the choice of prison, transportation or enlistment. When bad weather and local conditions produced unemployment, large numbers of recruits came forward. The best recruiting-sergeant was reputed to be Jack Frost, but his human counterpart cajoled many unsophisticated lads into the ranks by dangling an attractive cash-bounty, painting a glowing and quite misleading picture of army life, promising a smart uniform, a horse to ride, a sword to wield, free food, money to spend and a chance to see the world at the country's expense. His particular target was the gullible

and docile country lad raised by thrifty parents in a decent cottage home – they were always the most preferred type of recruit.

Having taken the irrevocable step of accepting the Queen's shilling, the recruit embarked upon a nightmare life of savage drill and remorseless bullying calculated to 'break' him by cowering and taming him into submission. This harsh treatment and the unhealthy living conditions inflicted upon young men of poor physique

Above: Trooper, 10th Hussars North-West Frontier 1879.

and low health standards, often from large and poor families prone to malnutrition and even rickets, caused the Army to have a death-rate many times higher than that of the civilian population.

When, through panic, stupidity or boredom, the soldier transgressed in even the most minor fashion, he was sentenced to periods of 'pack-drill' so prolonged and ferocious that he was reduced to a state of complete exhaustion. Sometimes it all became too much for him and he deserted – apprehended, he was flogged then branded on the upper-arm with a nee-

Right:
Guards Camel Detachment, Sudan 1884/5.

dle-device, gunpowder being rubbed in to make the letter 'D' permanent. A British soldier could still be flogged in 1881, and a few men were thus treated during the Second Afghan War 1878–80 for rendering themselves unfit for duty by drinking brandy stolen from medical stores. From 1859 the punishment was strictly reserved for certain classes of offence, and subsequently the Mutiny Act of 1868 restricted all corporal punishment to crimes committed on Active Service, but prolonged Parliamentary debates from 1876 to 1879 failed to abolish flogging altogether. The Army decreed that no man should be promoted to corporal without passing the lowest standard in the regimental school, and for the next ten years there were cases of regimental funds being used to provide inducements for soldiers to attend school. Not until the late 1880s did organised education get under way.

Soldiers with literary pretensions got into print. Private Charles Wickens of the 9th Regiment wrote an *Indian Mutiny Journal* in which he took exception to what Russell of *The Times* had said about the British soldier's inactivity in India:-

'Still, what he calls inactivity I call harassing duty. Suppose that Russell had been a common soldier instead of a correspondent. I fancy that I see him fully accoutred, falling in on parade with sixty rounds of ammunition, his rifle and bayonet weighing $11\frac{1}{2}$ lb, his haversack with two days' provisions in it and lastly a water-bottle slung by his side. Having imagined him to fall in on parade with his regiment he now marches off with it. The regiment halts after having gone over eleven miles of ground knee-deep in dust and almost dying for a drop of water. He is next put on picquet, where he remains till the next morning, when he is permitted to take his belts off while he washes his hands and face. And before he had been able to get a drop of coffee, the regiment is again on the move. Fresh ground is taken up either to the right or left or maybe we go a mile further, where there is a bridge and we are there to intercept them. Three or four days at a time are passed in this way. In all this marching out and in all weather and at all hours of the night or day was, in Mr. Russell's opinion, three months' ease – we were lying inactive at Nawabgunge. Would he not have sung a different song if he was there to have gone through the above? I think he would!'

Sergeant Tom Gowing of the 7th Royal Fusiliers, who wrote *A Soldier's Experience or A Voice From The Ranks*, recalls how, after the abortive British attack on the Redan the soldiers themselves accepted flogging as a punishment, old sweats being of the opinion that '... it serves him right ... saves guards on him too!' The Army Discipline Act of 1881 abolished flogging, replacing it on Active Service with Field Punishment No.1, when the convicted man was lashed to a gun wheel for a specified number of hours – a system still in use during the First World War.

Perhaps the greatest handicap under which the Victorian soldier laboured was being 'barrack-square bound', beset by severe and tedious discipline, spending most of his life in and around grim and grimy buildings or garrisoning some ancient fort or castle often situated in the heart of a crowded city. Crammed into these squalid barracks, each soldier had less than 300 cubic feet of space at a time when even convicts were allocated 1,000 cubic feet. Overcrowding and generally inadequate sanitary conditions provoked mortality rates much higher than the $7\frac{1}{2}$–9 deaths per 100 in civilians of military age – the Guards had 20 deaths per 1,000, Line Infantry 18 and cavalry 11. From consumption alone the Army had 18 deaths per 1,000

men compared to $3\frac{1}{2}$ per 1,000 among civilians.

Built in the 1850s, Aldershot Camp was claimed to be the last word in barrack construction, but was damp and draughty, lit by smelly oil lamps until replaced by flickering gas-jets; in the centre of the room, coal stoves only lighted in the coldest of weathers, baked those nearest them, while those on the fringes remained chilled. Hot water was unknown in the ablution huts sited, with primitive latrines, in the open outside the barrack room; during the night hours men relieved themselves in odorous tubs placed in soggy corners of the room. Every room was

Above: Infantry, Sudan 1884/5.

appallingly overcrowded with beds almost touching one another, iron cots folded during the day when the mattress – straw changed every three months – was neatly arranged with the pillow, pair of monthly changed sheets and four blankets, washed when they were noticeably filthy. Life was a constant battle against fleas and lice.

Food was plain and monotonous: a daily ration of 11 pounds of bread and 12 ounces of meat (including bone, fat and offal) appeared at midday as a stew, or a very infrequent roast; potatoes were always boiled and plentiful. Breakfast consisted of bread and biscuits (hard-tack) soaked in coffee and commonly called 'slingers'. In the late afternoon the last meal of the day was white bread (provided from the Canteen Fund) and a basin of tea. Until 1873, deductions were made from each man's pay to cover the cost of rations; the soldier provided his own plate and basin, used for soup, tea, coffee, beer and shaving-water. Meals were eaten in the barrack room, board and trestle tables being erected in the narrow alley between beds, where the men perched for lack of chairs. Overseas, much of the sickness that invariable affected British troops could be blamed on the abominable food provided by the Army and purchased from dubious private sources. Outdoors, over smoky fires amid dust and flies, unwashed native cooks transformed half-rotten meat and bad vegetables into unpalatable sickness-producing meals.

Material conditions for the soldier changed very slowly during Queen Victoria's reign. In 1845 the principle of a grant of a penny per day good-conduct pay for every five years service was affirmed, and two years later it was officially declared that no soldier should ever receive less than a penny per day actual cash. In 1854, the daily stoppage for a man's rations was

reduced from sixpence to fourpence halfpenny so that, at the outbreak of the Crimean War in that year, the soldier received a minimum of a shilling per day plus a penny per day beer money – from this total deduct fourpence halfpenny for rations, and from the remaining eightpence halfpenny came regimental stoppages and the cost of such necessaries as cleaning materials.

In 1860 a new scale of good conduct pay was introduced, ranging from a penny per day after three years' service up to sixpence per day after 28 years service. In 1865, the pay of a private of Infantry of the Line was thirteen pence a day – one shilling for wages and one penny for beer money, less eightpence halfpenny for rations, groceries and vegetables; from the remaining threepence halfpenny, the man had to pay for barrack damages, washing, renewal of forage-cap, a shell jacket, three shirts, a razor, brushes, soap, sponge and haversack. In 1867 an extra tuppence was added to the daily pay and recruiting improved at once. In 1870, good conduct pay was set within the man's reach after two years' service, a step that had become necessary in order to keep pace with the conditions of the new short-service. In 1893, a free daily ration of food was introduced which raised the daily rate of pay to one shilling – but the soldier ceased to receive beer money.

In 1876, a daily rate of tuppence per day for deferred pay was introduced, to give a man a start in civil life on entering the Army Reserve; the man would not receive the total sum of the deferred pay until he took his discharge.

In 1898, new regulations assured the private soldier of his full shilling a day, but instead of the tuppence per day deferred pay presented to the soldier on discharge, he was to get £1 for every year of service, up to a maximum of £12. At tuppence per day, deferred pay over a seven year period amounted to something like £20 – so the soldier lost again!

The Queen's Army was almost exclusively concerned with minor colonial campaigns involving small expeditions unmotivated by profound patriotism or thought for great national causes. Of course right was not always on the side of the British and the soldiers often fought and died to further the plans and plots of distant politicians. Lacking a Peninsula or a Sevastopol to stir the warlike emotions of either Army or public, now and then there was the stimulus of a hard-pressed garrison that had to be relieved, but in the main it was a seemingly ceaseless succession of small but hard-fought battles in alien terrains against fierce natives and hostile tropical conditions. Such hours of high excitement briefly punctuated weeks and months of soul-destroying boredom that could well have had a deadening effect upon the uneducated and initiative-dulled man in the ranks, but there is nothing to indicate that his undoubted character was spoilt or affected. Indeed, had his morale and quality been lowered he could not have been successful in this gamble for life or death against fierce and barbarous foes where the difference between outright victory and stalemate was annihilation. Men were quite ready to risk their lives rather than leave behind a wounded comrade because capture meant being slowly sliced to death by the sharp knives of the native women, or drowning as they squatted to urinate in the prostrate soldier's mouth, held open by a forked stick.

Like those before him and those who followed, the Victorian soldier possessed the quality of being cheerfully patient under the worst conditions; when reasonably comfortable he found constant grumbling to be the only conceivable way of expressing his feelings. Sent overseas solely to represent physical force, he invariably became a great moral force; despite hardships, sickness and boredom he was usually well behaved, reasonably honest and amazingly gentle as though his crude existence caused him innately to achieve self-respect free from self-consciousness. Throughout the Queen's reign, the scorned but disciplined soldier balanced deficiencies of physique and intellect with courage, endurance and humour to fight and conquer superior numbers of such natural warriors as Sikhs, Afghans, Zulus, Maoris, Pathans, Ghazis or Dervishes. The soldier's innate mercifulness rather than the obedience taught by training prevented any wanton slaughtering of defeated foes – as would be ably demonstrated by his descendants when being sniped and bombed in Palestine, Cyprus, Aden and Ireland. At the end of the Indian Mutiny, Sir Hugh Rose said in his final order: 'You have fought against the strong and you have protected the rights of the weak and defenceless, foes as well as friends. I have seen you in the ardour of combat preserve and place children out of harm's way. This is the discipline of Christian soldiers.' Such was the measure of respect for their conquerors that these warrior-races allowed themselves to be formed into military formations to work harmoniously and loyally in India, Africa, Asia, Borneo and the West Indies.

As the 19th century rolled on, military needs took the soldier ever farther from home, and his finest hours were spent away from his native land so that his triumphs, fortitude in adversity and patience under arduous conditions passed unnoticed. During decades of British colonial expansion his destiny was to meet an unhonoured and unsung, but often heroic

Above: At Kasr-el-Nil Barracks, in Cairo, General Grenfell takes the salute of the Guards, August 1898.

constitutional courage reflected in a burning universal desire for active service.

It is both wrong and unjust to credit success in these Victorian 'Small Wars' to the Martini-Henry rifle, the Gatling and the Screw-Gun. Victory was gained through the unremitting observance of regimental honour, tradition, spirit, and high standards of duty combining to produce first-class morale and comradeship. From commanding officer to lowly drummer-boy, every man in the regiment sought opportunities to win distinction and reputation, encouraged by the Victoria Cross being awarded for acts of outstanding gallantry and sheer cold-blooded courage, often with little military value beyond the raising of morale.

Every campaign was typical yet unique, their most remarkable feature being the men who fought them – the common soldier, the man-in-the-ranks – Kipling's immortal Ortheris, Mulvaney and Learoyd serve as typical representatives of them all. Obeying orders and doing their duty under the most arduous conditions, lacking knowledge of cause or reason, the British Regular soldiers carried out punitive expeditions, avenged wrongs, and engaged in political wars of expediency. Throughout the Victorian era, the British soldier fought and died amid inhospitable alien terrain where the difference between outright success and stalemate was annihilation. Drilled into blind obedience by harsh discipline, he displayed courage, endurance and humour, often under the most adverse conditions.

The history of the British Army poses one great truth – it is that in all the wars it has waged, whenever the British soldier has taken the field properly trained and well-led, adequately armed and supplied, he has never failed to respond wholeheartedly to all demands made upon him.

end, in a distant place with an unpronounceable name. For this the man in the ranks got little reward; some of his officers achieved great rewards and public acclaim – if they lived to enjoy them. For these officers a reputation for personal courage was the key to promotion – the British soldier has never lacked bravery and in the Victorian Army it was a quality pushed almost to excess by both officers and men who all shared a common trait of

4
Khaki & Red: The Victorian Soldier's Uniform

William IV believed that all British soldiers should wear red because this colour had been the mark of the British soldier since Elizabethan times. It is not known whether Queen Victoria shared her predecessor's belief, but for almost the first forty years of her reign she allowed her Army to proceed overseas and take the field arrayed in trappings identical with those they wore at her Coronation Procession – or exactly the same uniform as the soldier wore on Church Parade in a peaceful English garrison town. The colonial campaigns of the early 19th century were fought by men dressed in restricting scarlet tunics, trousers tightly strapped over Wellington boots, and a shako that provided little protection to head or neck. The soldier, particularly if he had served overseas, was aware that his uniform was completely unsuitable for work in the field; that active service required boots fit for marching, and that a peaked pillbox hat with a pocket handkerchief wrapped round it was little protection against a tropical sun. In the punctilious observation of past routines and traditions, soldiers saw their gorgeous uniforms reduced to rags and their gold lace shredded as they set about defeating Sikhs on dusty Indian plains, Kaffirs and Ashantis in African bush, and other assorted natives in jungles and mountains. And defeat them they did, although marching and fighting in tropical climates equipped and dressed very much as at Waterloo some forty or fifty years earlier, yet it was a period when it would have been a startling heresy to suggest that men be issued with suitable clothing for the conditions and the job in hand.

Harsh natural conditions forced adaptations of dangerously unsuitable clothing, as sheer wear and tear coupled with tactical requirements compelled clothing regulations to be ignored by commanding officers who, displaying more common sense than their masters in London, allowed men to replace tattered uniforms with more suitable clothing. The advantages gained by natives fighting on their own terrain were partly off-set by the British troops adopting, when possible, garments so coloured as to aid concealment; during the Kaffir War of 1852 when uniforms were torn to rags after a few days patrol duty in the forest, they were replaced with whatever came to hand. Men of the 6th Regiment were described as having '... red coats patched with leather, canvas and cloth of all colours; straw hats or wide-awakes; long beards, tattered trousers and broken boots revealing stockingless feet'. Colonel Michael, commanding a regiment during this campaign, went into action with his shirt-sleeves tucked up to his elbows, his wide-awake hat cocked on one side, strong Blücher boots on his feet and corduroy trousers on his legs.

Throughout history, the British soldier has always set about modifying his uniform to suit his fancy or his needs. During Marlborough's campaigns, the long cassock-shaped scarlet coats reaching below the knees were found cumbrous and inconvenient, so the fronts were folded back and buttoned to the middle of the back below the waist, leaving the legs free – those two buttons on the back of coats remained long after they had ceased to serve any useful purpose. Two hundred years later, during the First World War, khaki greatcoats were too long-skirted for the muddy waterlogged trenches of Flanders, so they were ruthlessly cut short, to produce the British 'Warm' overcoat.

The Crimean War proved that a smartly dressed puppet was not necessarily best suited for a long campaign in an adverse climate. When Raglan led his expedition to Russia, British uniforms were recovering from the extravagances of the pre-Victorian period, although still completely impractical and utterly unsuited to the rigours of the Crimean winter. Regiments left England for the Black Sea dressed as though for a parade in Hyde Park; some men did not even have greatcoats; the Guards wore bearskin caps and Line Infantry the 'Albert' shako and scarlet coatee. The Light and Heavy Brigades charged at Balaclava wearing tight and restricting full-dress uniform – their only concession to warfare being the discontinuation of the head-dress plume. This was soon to change, and a few weeks after leaving England a cholera-ridden army shambled from Aladyn in columns of wild and ragged bearded men, marching with dragging feet, tattered and

torn uniforms covering their bent frames. As the harsh Russian winter progressed, the short-waisted coatees worn by the infantry afforded little protection; shakos were replaced by knitted woollen caps; soldiers patched tattered uniforms with multi-coloured materials, and local garments were pressed into service until the soldier was a far cry from the smart man who had marched to the docks at Portsmouth. Overcoats of local purchase and fur garments worn with long boots made him look like a bulky teddy-bear. The unfortunate Hussar, expected to wear his pelisse as an overcoat, suffered greatly because the ship carrying them was sunk in Balaclava harbour.

The storm of public criticism aroused by Russell and others from the front forced the authorities to make concessions and improvements. In 1855, the short infantry coatee with the useless tails was replaced by a double-breasted tunic with deep skirts which afforded protection to the body. By early November before the next winter, every British soldier was equipped with a fine winter kit: an excellent tweed coat lined throughout with rabbit or cat-skin, a larger and still warmer sheepskin coat, two pairs of thick worsted drawers, two jerseys, a pair of worsted gloves, a worsted cholera-belt, a pair of long waterproofed boots, a waterproof sheet, a pair each of worsted stockings and socks, and a sealskin cap that could be turned down to cover the neck and ears.

Always more practical than the Home Army, the Army in India began to make concessions to climatic conditions during the Second Sikh War, but even more so during the Indian Mutiny ten years later. Seeking comfort in battle, officers and sometimes soldiers were permitted to wear either a sun-helmet or a forage-cap with a pugaree – a thin muslin scarf –

wrapped around it, with the ends falling down behind to keep the sun off the back of the neck and spine. A peaked cap with a havelock hanging down to protect the neck was worn, and some units wore white linen shirts or white hot-climate jackets. For some years regulations provided for every soldier on arrival in India to be equipped with additional articles of clothing – 4 white jackets; 1 pair of English summer trousers; 5 pairs of white trousers; 5 white shirts; 2 check shirts, and 1 pair white braces – all made on the spot and composed of materials best suited for the climate. On alternate years during his stay in India, the British soldier was provided with a tunic and shell-jacket; in the year in which the tunic was not issued, the difference in the value of the two articles was paid by the soldier and expended by his commanding officer for his benefit on any article suited to the climate of the station. Although the force sent out to India in 1857 had been issued with white cotton helmets and forage-cap covers, Highlanders marched to relieve Lucknow in feather bonnets and white spats. At the siege of Delhi, newly-arrived British infantry units wearing 'Home' dress, with the sole concession of a white cap-cover, mingled with khaki-clad Indian native regiments, and even fought mutinous Sepoys who were wearing the same clothing.

In India, the time-honoured scarlet of the British Army was slowly being replaced by uniforms of khaki – the Persian word for 'dust' or 'stone' coloured; sometimes it was called 'khakee' and defined as 'ash coloured'. It is probable that khaki was originally less yellow and more grey than it later became; probably the original khaki dye was curry powder. During the Mutiny a few British regiments such as the 32nd and 52nd Light Infantry dyed their white clothing

with such substances as coffee, curry powder, mulberry juice, etc. The First Bengal European Fusiliers (later the Royal Munster Fusiliers) campaigned without coats in their grey shirts, earning the nick-name of the 'Dirty Shirts'. In some regiments men were allowed to purchase, at their own expense, sun helmets as worn by their officers.

When, in December 1857, General Sir Hugh Rose assumed command of the Central Indian Field Force, one of his first measures was to provide the infantry with loose khaki clothing and, after the fall of Jhansi in 1858, the 71st Regiment wore khaki blouses and overalls with a head-dress that provided good protection from the sun.

The much publicised distress experienced by British troops in the intense heat of the Indian sun, coupled with Parliamentary criticism of those regimental officers who compelled their soldiers to swelter in red cloth, made inevitable new rulings concerning the issue of light summer clothing. Advised that khaki was even better suited than white as a material for clothing in the hot season, on 21 May 1858 the Adjutant-General issued an order:

'With the concurrence of the Government, the Commander-in-Chief is pleased to direct that white clothing shall be discontinued in the European regiments of the Honourable Company's Army; that for the future the summer clothing of the European soldiers shall consist of two suits of "khakee" corresponding in pattern and material with the clothing recently sanctioned for the Royal Army of England. Corps are to be permitted to wear out serviceable summer clothing of the old pattern now in use; but in regiments in which this clothing requires to be renewed, the new pattern now established is to be introduced without delay. Commanding officers will take steps to obtain patterns from Regiments of Her Majesty's Service. A complete suit, including cap-cover, should not exceed in cost 4 to 12 rupees. The summer clothing now authorised will be supplied from the Clothing Agency of the Presidency to all recruits of the Company's Service arriving at Calcutta between 1st February and 1st October, to be issued with the least possible delay after arrival of the recruits.'

Unfortunately the new coloured clothing came in so many different shades and blotchy hues that the men complained that they felt 'scruffy' and refused to 'walk out' in the new clothing, spending rather their evenings in the canteen, which lead to increase in drunkenness. Eventually it went out of use for several years, except on the North-West Frontier where it was worn by such units as the Guides. White drill became the normal summer dress in India, but khaki returned for the Afghan War of 1878.

Highland regiments, in their distinctive but highly vulnerable uniform, probably suffered more than other infantry regiments. During the Crimean winter they found the kilt too cold, so it was replaced by breeks and only appeared on defaulters' parades. According to a contemporary writer: 'if the gallant Highlanders ever wore the kilt it was for punishment. Breeks and blanket-gaiters and any leggings over them were the wear of our Scottish Zouaves.' Before this, in the early 1850s, when the 42nd Regiment (the Black Watch) were in Bermuda, the damp chill tropical nights caused them to be ordered to hand in their plaids, kilts and bonnets in exchange for duck pantaloons and round hats, hated by all ranks. The feather bonnet gave way to a cheap and trashy hat of coarse felt which, its shape destroyed by the first rainfall, stuck close to the head and afforded no protection against the sun. The men asserted that the normal bonnet, of thick wool covered with feathers, was a complete protection against the tropical sun, besides being a warm and unconventional night-cap. The new dress quickly proved to be completely unsuitable for local conditions – the pantaloons when soaked by the frequent rains clung to the legs and thighs, being very difficult to dry. Although mosquitoes were a great trouble to kilt wearers, when wet kilt and hose were taken off and wrung out, they could be immediately worn again in perfect safety. All ranks were delighted to get back into the kilt when they returned to the British Isles.

Throughout the Victorian era British cavalry were constantly handicapped by tight and unserviceable clothing, slippery saddles and unsuitable arms. Perhaps no weapon could be wielded really effectively unless the cavalrymen were suitably clothed in a simply designed uniform lacking such unnecessary appendages as plumes, sabretaches, sheepskins, and shabracques that dangled around both horse and rider. Doctor Andrew Fergusson, Inspector-General of Military Hospitals, ridiculed the '... foreign fooleries so laced and looped and braided of the Hussar; the woman's muff upon his head was something like a red jellybag on the top and the richly decorated

Right: Field Service Equipment Pattern 1882.

31

Left: Equipment worn during the First Sudan Campaign, 1884. Top, 4th Dragoon Guards; below, Guards Camel Regiment.

pelisse waving empty, sleeves and all ... an abuse and prostitution of the English character'. During the Kaffir War of 1852, wearing tightly strapped-down overalls, the 12th Royal Lancers were frequently in action against superior numbers of Basuto horsemen, well-mounted warriors armed with battle-axes and assegais and reputed to be 'equal to the Cossacks'. Over very bad going, troopers' horses fell and, the enemy pressing closely, would not stand to be remounted – if a comrade failed to return to hold the horse, the

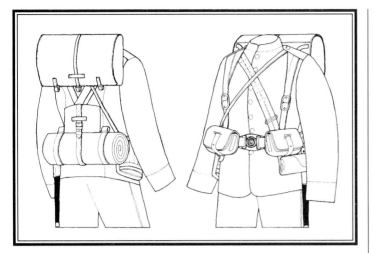

Above: Service Equipment Pattern, 1888, known as the 'Slade-Wallace' Equipment, parts of which, such as the waist belt, are still in use.

dismounted man, prevented by tight overalls from mounting without assistance, was inevitably killed. Even as late as the Afghan War of 1878 cavalrymen were so hampered by their leg gear, overalls and tight riding-boots that they were kept in their saddles as much as possible. In 1879, two famous cavalry regiments in Zululand, arrayed in all the trappings of a Royal procession, very soon saw their gold lace in shreds and their gorgeous tunics in ribbons. Before that they undoubtedly presented a vivid contrast to the Irregular Horse led by Buller and Bettington.

In 1859 the infantryman's tunic was changed to a single-breasted garment, cut quite full and retaining deep skirts. The new tunics were very comfortable with a collar much reduced in height. Cavalry were also given a new tunic, that of the Hussars having less braid across the chest than previously. In 1862 the leather stock, which had so restricted the neck, was abolished, being replaced by a small black leather tab. Highland troops adopted a doublet with elaborate cuffs and skirt flaps piped with white braid; Highland stockings of stitched tartan were replaced by softer knitted hose. The infantryman's overcoat was greatly improved in quality and, in

1869, was fitted with a detachable cape.

French successes in the Crimea started a fashion for their style of military clothing and a new pattern of tunic and shako were introduced, the tall 'Albert' shako of the infantry and Light Dragoon being reduced in height and size. With the passing of the years it continued to be reduced in height until 1877, following Prussian military successes, the shako was replaced by the pickelhaube and all troops, except Highlanders, were issued with a blue cloth spiked helmet – the last full-dress headgear for British Infantry of the Line. Rifle regiments were issued with the helmet but it was soon replaced by a black fur cap; Lowland regiments were issued with a stiffened bonnet, the Kilmarnock. Alone of all Line Regiments, the Scottish Rifles and the Highland Light Infantry retained versions of the shako. The Hussars retained their busby, though of slightly reduced size, and the Lancers their cap; the Heavy Cavalry helmet had its decorations simplified. Black plumes were replaced by coloured ones. The Field Artillery replaced their fur cap with the same helmet, but with a ball instead of a spike.

In the 1860s, soldiers fighting the Maoris in New Zealand were issued with a uniform better adapted for their task than the usual redcoat; for the Ashanti campaign of 1873, the Black Watch wore sun helmets and grey tweed tunics. In Canada, troops were issued with fur caps, mitts and warm coats. The traditional scarlet tunic was last worn in action by British troops at the Battle of Ginnis in the Sudan, fought on the last day-but-one of 1885.

British soldiers serving abroad were universally wearing khaki by the end of the 19th century, but as soon as a regiment returned to Great Britain, the unsightly clothing was handed-in to the stores and out came the scarlet, blue and green uniforms, the plumes, pennons, the schapska and sabretache, busby and bearskin. The South Africa War of 1899–1902 saw the beginning of the end of this practice, but even so the British soldier marched off to fight the Boers in a reasonable khaki drill uniform, but wearing a helmet that could charitably be said to have been designed for almost any purposes except protection from the tropical sun!

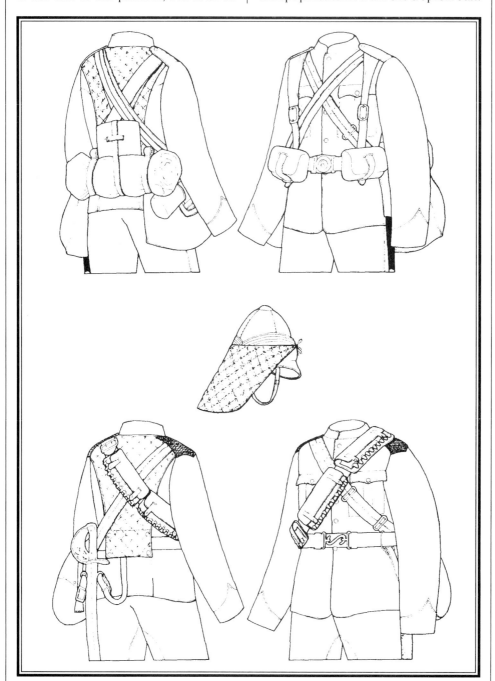

Left: Equipment worn during the Second Sudan Campaign, 1898. Top, infantry; below, cavalry (21st Lancers). Note the quilted cotton spine pads and neck covers for the helmet.

5
The Victorian Soldier's Weapons

The twenty years that followed Waterloo saw few changes in the armament of the British soldier, but from 1840 new and superior weapons were placed in his hands every fifteen or twenty years. The flint-lock musket that had served the British infantry-man for two centuries averaged 270 hits per 1,000 shots and always threw the bullet high – Sir Charles Napier told his troops in Sind: 'The first duty of a soldier is obedience; his second – to fire low.' It was hardly worth firing at any target smaller than the side of a barn from a distance of 100 yards. In 1840 the percussion-lock musket (later improved by being breech-loaded) began to replace the old 'Brown Bess' and, for the first time in the history of the British Army, the calibre of muskets, carbines and rifles was the same, so that one pattern of ammunition served for all. Within 50 years, the rifle was destined to bring greater changes to warfare than had been seen throughout the entire period from Naseby to Waterloo. It was a revolutionary change and a great improvement because the new weapon averaged 385 hits per 1,000 shots and misfires were reduced to $4^1/2$ per 1,000 shots against the 411 per 1,000 of the flint-lock musket. The percussion-musket was first used by the British Army in action by Marines at the capture of

Canton in 1841. Had the new musket reached India at the time it was first issued in England, the disastrous war in Afghanistan might well have taken a different turn. Both this campaign and the 1840 war in China were fought with the old flint-lock musket.

Early in 1852 a number of Minié rifles were sent to South Africa for active service trials against the Kaffirs. The Minié was a muzzle-loading weapon with a wide bore ($7/10$-inch); its three grooves with a spiral twist of 1 in 72 inches gave rotation to a heavy conical bullet possessing great smashing power. Sighted up to 900 yards, it was reasonably accurate and, although a muzzle-loader, it was a great advance upon the old smooth-bore musket. Using a white target, 6 feet high and 3 feet wide, it was usual to achieve 2 hits in 5 shots at from 500 to 800 yards, while at 900 yards 7 shots usually produced 1 hit. The initial distribution allowed for only six men in each company (usually the best shots) to be armed with this new rifle, and on numerous occasions at ranges of 1,200–1,300 yards, small groups of Kaffirs were dispersed and some killed. Being a long rifle, it had the advantage of being effective with a fixed bayonet.

In the same war, the King's Royal Rifle Corps used the Brunswick percussion-rifle, a weapon that took so long to load that each man was issued with a few rounds of smooth-bore ammunition for emergencies.

When the Crimean war broke out in 1854, the Army were being re-equipped with the Minié rifle, but the war was fought primarily with the old smooth-bore musket. In use at the same time was the Enfield rifle, which ultimately superseded the Minié. Weighing only 8 pounds 14 ounces as against the 14 pounds of the 'Brown Bess', the Enfield needed a far closer fit of cartridge and ball. In order to be quickly rammed down the 39-inch barrel, the cartridges were encased in greased paper and their ends had to be bitten off so that the powder could be poured down the barrel. The remainder, containing the wad and bullet, was then forced home with the ram-rod, the bullet also having to be lubricated to enable it to be driven down the rifle without undue effort. The Indian Mutiny is said to have been triggered-off because the caste-conscious Sepoys of the Bengal army believed the cartridges to be greased with beef-fat or hog-lard. Strenuous efforts equipped the British troops in the Abyssinian expedition of 1868 with the new Snider rifle, a breech-loader which, with bayonet attached, was

72½ inches long. By 1869 all the Regulars, plus 16,000 militia, had been so equipped.

In the same year improved equipment was issued that allowed the greatcoat (carried on the shoulders), and the two ammunition pouches (worn on the waist-belt and each containing 20 rounds) supported by a pair of braces connected at the belt at both ends, to balance each other. Hung from separate slings, the haversack and water-bottles still constricted the chest. From 1873 to 1889, Slade-Wallace equipment was in use, where the valise or pack was carried in a curious manner, suspended on the buttocks, with supporting straps attached to the front buckles of the braces. Black pouches were worn on the white equipment, probably because the old cartouche box had been black so as not to show greasy finger-marks from the lubricant on the paper cartridges. When the Martini-Henry rifle was issued in 1871, an extra pouch carried another 30 rounds. During the Egyptian campaigns of 1882–5 illustrations show the infantryman wearing his equipment with ammunition pouches, bayonet, haversack and water–bottle, and only a mess–tin in a black cover on his back, strapped on where the

Below: The Martini-Henry rifle; mechanism and bayonet, 1871.

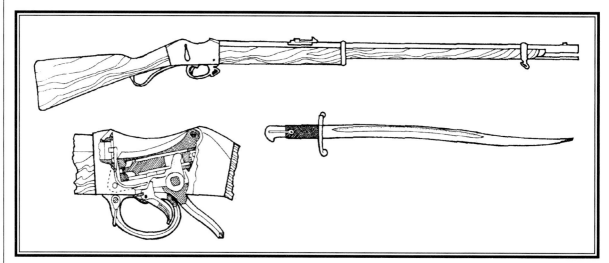

braces crossed. Because of the heat, packs were often not carried on the march, and of course greatcoats were unnecessary in the Egyptian summer.

In 1869 trials began of a new, hammerless .45 single-loader, the Martini-Henry, which ejected the cartridge case by a lever behind the trigger guard; it fired a heavy bullet with great stopping power. Its recoil was correspondingly violent and black powder was still used. The Martini-Henry, far superior to any arm previously issued to the British soldier, was easy to operate, quick to reload and reckoned to be accurate up to 800 yards. With bayonet attached it was 5 feet 11½ inches long. First widely used on active service in Africa and Afghanistan, the Martini-Henry, a weapon with a small bore, great range, low trajectory and superior accuracy, has been claimed to be the earliest general issue of a shoulder arm that could compete successfully with the longbow of the Hundred Years War so far as range, rapidity of firing and robustness were concerned. Every earlier firearm, even the famous 'Brown Bess', had been in some degree inferior to the master-weapon of Crecy, Poitiers and Agincourt.

At this time there were several types of sword-bayonet, some with long wavy blades, but the ancient triangular-bladed type still predominated. In 1878 a new and longer bayonet was issued to the infantry, with a series of brass studs upon the scabbard.

In 1881, the rifles used in the British service were the Martini-Henry and the Snider-Enfield, the Artillery were issued with carbines by the same makers; the cavalry were equipped with the Westley-Richards carbine. With the new and improved firearms came a new system of drill described in *Field Exercises and Evolutions of Infantry*, specially issued in April 1877.

In about 1860, General Sir Samuel Browne, V.C., who had lost an arm and required a more convenient method of carrying his sword and revolver, invented the Sam Browne belt. It came into general use for officers during the wars of 1870 to 1880, and is now worn also by Warrant Officers Class I, and has been adopted by nearly all the armies of the world.

Invented in 1889, the Lee-Metford magazine rifle, using smokeless cordite and with a magazine holding 8 rounds (which had to be loaded one at a time) was the weapon which, in Kitchener's Dongola Campaign, killed or wounded about 25,000 Sudanese at the battle of Omdurman, not a single native closing nearer than 150 yards. This, despite the fact that the Lee-Metford bullet drilled a hole even through bone without bringing down or stopping the rush of a fanatic such as a 'Fuzzy-Wuzzy' or a Zulu, because of the pencil-thin diameter of the bullet. Nevertheless, the Lee-Metford revolutionised warfare because it banished the old problems of the target being obscured by a cloud of black smoke after each volley and, at the same time, revealing the position of the firer.

From about 1895 the .303 short Lee-Enfield rifle, with slight modifications, served the British soldier faithfully through both World Wars. British craftsmen can derive much credit from the production of a firearm that proved itself on many battlefields to be the best of its kind.

During the 19th century hardly any soldier, except an infantry private, could escape having to carry a sword of one pattern or another. In the British Army, artillerymen, engineers, bandsmen, pioneers and even medical auxiliaries wore them. The Highland regiments wore an extra-special type, the broadsword. In 1853 it was laid down that all cavalry troopers be armed with the same pattern of sword, imported in quantity from Germany.

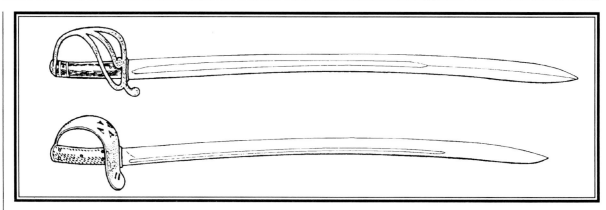

During the fierce battles in Egypt against the Mahdi and his Dervishes in the 1880s many of these weapons failed completely – blades and hilts bent or even broke, not only in action but through the ordinary wear and tear of campaigning. In the Boer War, the sword worn by the cavalry proved quite useless in action and it was not until after this period that a really first-rate weapon was designed and turned out in quantity.

The terrain and the conditions under which Victoria's small wars were fought only allowed the use of light artillery – Britain won her colonial wars with 13-pounder field guns, and mountain guns broken down into components and carried by mules. The hillmen of India's North-West Frontier said that what they feared was '...not the child-rifle but the devil guns, which killed half a dozen men with one shot (shell) which burst and threw up splinters as deadly as the shots themselves'.

In the early colonial wars, gun-metal was often preferred for artillery used in tropical or mountainous areas. For the Bhutan expedition of 1865, 3-pounder brass smooth-bores, machined-out to 3 inches in the bore and rifled on the French system, were issued as the 7-pounder Mk I. Proving too heavy, a 7-pounder Mk II was produced and adopted by both Army and Navy. All brass guns were withdrawn from service in 1874. In 1881, breech-loading guns for the Royal Horse Artillery and field brigades were issued for service at Woolwich. As far as was practicable, being breech-loaders, these guns were constructed on the model of the muzzle-loading 13-pounder, deemed

Above: British cavalry swords for other ranks. Top, 1853 Pattern; below, 1864 Pattern.

Below: British cavalry swords for other ranks. Top, 1885 pattern; below, 1899 pattern.

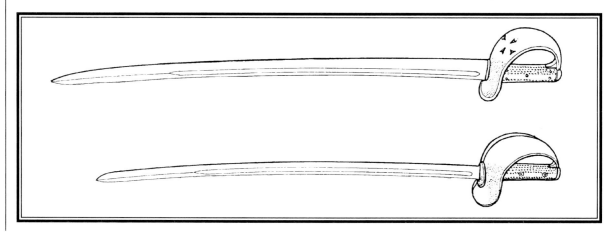

Above: E Battery, B Brigade Royal Horse Artillery, decorated for distiguished conduct at the Battle of Maiwand during the Second Afghan War.

Right: The 9pdr rifled muzzle-loading field gun c.1882

to be the finest specimen of British ordnance. They were 3 inches in calibre at the bore and weighed only 8¼ cwt. The gun was mainly of steel with bronze fittings.

Repeatedly, accounts of these small colonial wars mention the mountain batteries which brought the use of mule transport to the point of perfection. Their officers claimed that they could take their guns anywhere a man could go, and they did so. Apparently blessed with hawk-like vision, they could pick out the lone Afridi sniper on the distant hillside who was annoying the advance with his stolen modern rifle. The mountain guns used in Abyssinia in 1868

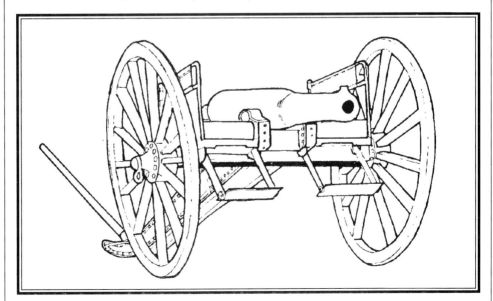

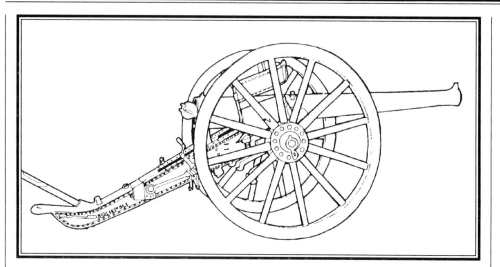

Left: The 12pdr rifled breech-loading field gun c.1890.

weighed about 150 pounds, but were later superseded by an almost identical piece weighing 200 pounds whose barrel was 3 feet 2 inches long. Two kinds of iron cradle were used, one taking the gun with its muzzle to the rear, and one the carriage, breast to the front. In 1880, the famous 'screw-gun' was introduced – made in two pieces which screwed together, this gun was later immortalised by Kipling. The gun itself weighed about 400 pounds and each mule carried a weight of about 300–320 pounds.

An early type of machine-gun, invented by Doctor Gatling of Chicago, was used in the Afghan War and also in Egypt. It consisted of a number of rifle barrels bound together like a faggot and mounted on wheels, with a firing mechanism worked by turning a handle similar to that of a barrel-organ. It was not a great success as it usually jammed at critical moment – prompting Sir Henry Newbolt to write:

Below: The 6in breechloading howitzer c.1900.

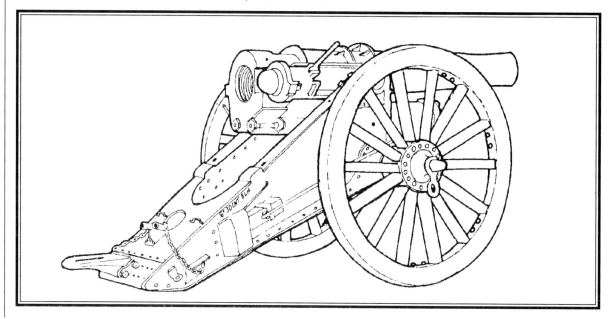

Right: A Gatling gun. **Far right:** A Nordenfelt gun.

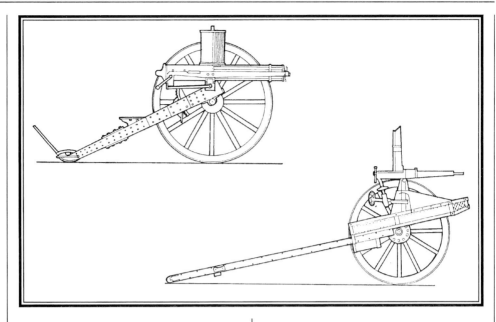

Below: An Egyptian Army mule battery in action.

'The sand of the desert is sodden red,
Red with the wreck of a square that
  broke.
The Gatling's jammed and the
  Colonel's dead,
And the regiment's blind with dust and
  smoke.'

In 1880, the Admiralty decided to adopt the Nordenfelt 4-barrelled gun, which fired twelve solid steel shot per second, for use in the Navy to repel torpedo-boat attacks. It was stated that this weapon was selected, after a series of exhaustive experiments, in

preference to the Gatling or Hotchkiss revolving cannon. In July 1883, the same 5-barrelled Nordenfelt gun, mounted on an ordinary infantry carriage, was adopted as an auxiliary weapon for infantry. The Gardner gun, another weapon of similar construction, was used during the Egyptian War. None of these 'machine-guns' was particularly efficient until 1883, when Hiram Maxim, an American, invented the first automatic gas-operated machine-gun, which, with slight improvements, became the Vickers gun. Maxim was also the inventor of the Pom-Pom used during the Second Boer War, which fired belts of 1-pound shells.

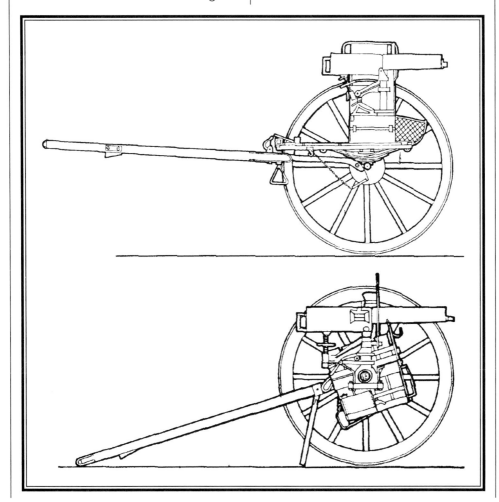

Left: A Maxim machine-gun. Top, mounted on a cavalry carriage; below, mounted on an infantry carriage.

PART TWO

THE 'GREAT GAME': THE VICTORIAN NIGHTMARE

Afridis and Khyber Pass Tribesmen, 1870.

6
Indian Version

In Britain the Victorian Era in Britain was marked by the conviction that British imperial policy and the possession of India – the Jewel in the Crown – were inseparable reasons for the existence and sustenance of the Empire and a major right for Britain to regard herself as a World Power. From the moment when, in 1798, the young and currently successful Napoleon Bonaparte proposed to the French Directory that France should strike at the main source of Britain's wealth by occupying Egypt and threatening the route to India (and thereby incidentally alerted British statesmen to the importance of Egypt), British troop movements throughout the world were mainly governed by the long-term defence of India. In justifying the continued British presence on the North-West Frontier of India, British and Indian Governments claimed they had no other choice, believing that the Frontier played the same part in the strategic defence of Empire as did Gibraltar and the Suez Canal, in that it was a natural barrier or boundary to a Russian invasion of India. In the late 19th century, British military operations and the presence in the Sudan and on the North-West Frontier of India were directed against the possibility of a Russian invasion through the North-West Frontier, and from the French – or any other Power – invasion through the Suez Canal, the road to India.

The 19th-century Anglo-Russian contretemps over Central Asia has been called 'The Great Game' – a wry title for a lengthy struggle which, at times, approached open conflict and generated a pervasive paranoia among British policy-makers, dramatically reflected time and time again on the North-West Frontier of India. Holding India, Britain had no further ambitions in that area, but was intensely suspicious of Russian motives in the relentless eastward conquest of Central Asia. Hindsight indicates however that Russia never revealed that same feverishness to conquer India as the British displayed to prevent it occurring. The pace of the 'Great Game' began to accelerate in 1868 when Russia occupied Bokhara, the possession of which – together with Samarkand – narrowed to a mere 400 miles the gap between the adventurous Russians and the Punjab Frontier Force patrolling the trans-Indian hills. Frontier policies were re-assessed and the geography of the area was closely studied during the development of counter-moves to Russian expansion, including the necessary establishment of a British presence in Kabul which, in its turn, led to war with Afghanistan within a decade. During this period, an Afghan Regular army with Russian-

Above: In the mid-1880s, Russian troops on the march towards the Afghan border halt at the town of Baku on the Caspian Sea.

trained artillery officers, defeated a British force at Maiwand in July 1880.

These were days when Russian movements on the northern Afghan frontier aroused a crisis in the 'Great Game' by an apparent threat of invasion of India – which could have precipitated the First World War three decades ahead of schedule. At this time, Russian intensity of purpose in Central Asia aroused alarming fears that their next objective could be Afghanistan, perhaps followed by an invasion of India? The nightmare scenario pictured a Russian-backed Persian occupation of Herat, then advances through Kabul, until the British and Indian forces on the frontier found themselves facing a large allied army of Russians, Afghans and Persians.

The area remained turbulent for the next twenty years, with diplomatic and political manoeuvres between the two Powers holding-off a contiguous British-Russian border in Central Asia, to a background of increasingly fierce campaigns against the militant tribesmen. This culminated in the biggest outbreak of all between 1895 and 1898, followed immediately by the war against the Boers in South Africa, leading to a British loss of international face, which encouraged Russia to announce the opening of diplomatic relations with Afghanistan. By 1903 it seemed that the 'Great Game' was about to be won – on the North-West Frontier where it had begun, with the British still in possession. However, it vanished dramatically from the political gaming-tables in London, Delhi and Moscow when the Russians, ignominiously defeated in their 1905 war with Japan, realised that ambitious Germany was the real future foe and that Britain would be a useful ally against the Germans.

7
The Tribesmen of the North-West Frontier of India

From the moment of the annexation of the Punjab in 1849, the British and Indian Armies were brought into contact with martial races, all armed and apparently careless of their lives, whose lawlessness provoked countless campaigns and expeditions for a hundred years, and which were still causing problems at the time of Independence in 1948.

It was quickly realised that most trouble came from a 400-mile long, 100-mile wide strip of wild and mountainous territory known as the North-West Frontier which was to become the sole territory in the British Empire never fully conquered. It was a terrible country, harsh, relentless and jagged, with rocky and precipitous peaks and serrated ridges, narrow passes that penned-up the heat, and dry icy high ground. This was a perfect natural arena for ambush and sniping by tribesmen with deadly matchlocks hidden amid the heat of the hillsides, waiting their chance to pick-off stragglers or to tumble down in a fanatical rush, ready to die for Mohammed. Every tribe – and there were plenty of them – under the generic name of Pathans, had different characteristics and methods of warfare, yet all shared a common militancy and displayed identical traits of being disdainfully courageous, marvellous natural fighters in their own familiar terrain, and first-class marksmen.

The struggle for existence in such a barren country produced men of great physical endurance, who respected no authority and were extremely truculent. They were, as John Lawrence said '… men of predatory habits, careless and impatient of control …' and it made no difference to them whose control it was – after 1849 they shifted their belligerent stance against the Sikhs and concentrated on the British. Of all the many races of fighting men encountered by the British in the Victorian period, none were as consistently hostile or better fighters than the Pathans of this territory. Tall, hawk-eyed, bedecked with matchlocks and knives, keen as hawks and cruel as leopards, the Pathans were Pushtu-speaking Eastern Afghans of mixed ethnic origin, divided into many tribes, sub-tribes and clans; since the 10th century militant (if not always orthodox) followers of Islam, these hill-dwellers had controlled the rugged mountainous territory astride what is now the Afghan/Pakistan border. Their tribal sections, each with its *malik* (headman), were composed of blood relatives in a little community of separate dwellings, several of these sections formed a clan (*khel*) and the various *khel*s constituted the tribe, each having a *khan* or *arbab*.

Above: Two Afghans, clad in their winter dress, lurking in the foothills of the Koord-Kubal Pass to snipe at British troops.

Of the Pathan tribes, the Ilaszai Yusufzais composed of the Hassanzais, the Akazais and the Mada Khel inhabited the Black Mountains, east of the Indus and British territory northwest of Abbottabad, a 30-mile long narrow ridge about 8,000 feet above sea-level, surmounted by high peaks and thickly wooded country with deep and narrow passes between large spurs. The Ilaszai Yusufzais consisted of the Bunerwals of the Buner Valley, the Chagarzais of the Indus Valley at the northern end of the Black Mountains, and the Malikazais of the Dir and Panjkora Valley. In Chumla and the Indus Valley lived the Mandan

Yusufzais, formed of the Utmanzais and the Usmanzais. Allied Tribes were Swatis of the Swat Valley; Utman Khel of the Lower Swat Valley; Mamunds of the tumbling mountains of the Bajaur; Gaduns, who ruled between Chumla and the Indus Valleys, and Mohmands of the Kabul Valley, whose frontier was only twenty miles from Peshawar, and who gave more trouble than any other tribe in the district.

About 30,000 strong, the Afridi tribe with its numerous clans was the largest and most turbulent on the Frontier, and probably the best fighters. Among their most truculent clans were the Kuki Khels of the Rajgal Valley and the Zakka Khels of the Maidan, Bara and Bazar Valleys, the last named said to be '... the greatest thieves, housebreakers, robbers and raiders among all the Khyber clans, their word or promise never being believed or trusted by their Afridi brethren without a substantial security being taken for its fulfilment' (Warburton). A leading Afridi clan were the Orakzais of Southern Tirah and Samana Ridge, not as well-armed or as warlike, nevertheless numerous British expeditions had to go out against them; after the last in 1891, forts were built in their territory and garrisoned by Sikhs, traditional enemies of the Pathans. Also in the Maidan and Bara Valleys were the Malikdin Khel, Kambar Khel, Kamar Khel and Sipah Khel; the Aka Khel inhabited Warran and the Bara. The Dam Khel lived between Peshawar and Kohat, and the Zaimukhts north of Thai in Kurram Valley; the Jowaki Afridis in the Kohat Pass, while the Ghilzais exacted toll on numerous all-important mountain passes into India. Also there were the Turis of the Kurram Valley, the Mullagoris and Shinwaris of the Khyber, and the Khattacks of Kohat.

Lying between Kurram and Zhob, touching the Afghan frontier on the west and north-west, Waziristan is rugged, mountainous and barren, and scored by narrow ravines whose gorges (*tangis*) form natural defensive positions. Its principal tribes, the Darwesh Khel and the Mahsuds (known collectively as Wazirs) are perhaps the fiercest of all North-West Frontier tribes, being likened to wolves or panthers and officially recognised as '... the earliest, most inveterate and most incorrigible of all the robbers of the border'. The Mahsuds, it was reported, '... cannot be reformed and induced to relinquish their old ingrained habits of murdering, raising and thieving by

anything short of permanent occupation of their country'. Their rock-citadels were jumping-off points for endless raids on settled districts to the east, whose position was likened to that of early French settlers in Canada – '... who always moved about in constant dread of the Iroquois tomahawks'. Other Wazir tribes or clans were the Dawaris of the Tochi Valley, the Bhitannis of the hill country near Bannu and Tank; and the Shiranis of Takht-i-Suliman.

On the west bank of the Indus was Khelat, populated by non-Pathan Baluchi tribes, Brahuis, Bozdars, Bugtis, Gurchanis, Kasranis, Kehtrans, Khosas, Lagharis, Marris and Mazaris – more law-abiding but no less truculent than the Frontier clans. Other occasional opponents of the British were the slant-eyed, Mongol-descended Hazara tribesmen from the Bamian Valley; the Ghazis, mounted irregulars and fanatical Muslims who sought glory by dying in battle, wielding curved tulwars and fighting under the green flags of Islam. And the Hindustani fanatics, the only tribesmen who made trouble during the Mutiny of 1857, who lurked on the slopes of the Black Mountains on the northern Yusufzai frontier. They were a colony of Muslim refugees of the Wahabi sect from India, originally founded in 1820 by Sayid Ahmad Shah of Bareilly, killed in an unsuccessful *jihad* (holy war) called to eject the Sikhs from the Punjab before changing their objective to ousting the British. In 1895 a major campaign was fought against the northern tribes – the Chitralis of Chitral District; the Chilasis of Chilas District; the Kanjutis of the Kanjut Valley and the Kohistanis of Chicharga and Nila Naddi Valleys.

Without exception, internecine warfare and the raiding of Frontier villages formed the major part of the lives of all these tribes and clans; it seemed

Above: A group of Dawaris, natives of the Torchi country.

Right: Mohammed Din, an Ummer Kheyl, of Durunta.

Their battles were fought in an extraordinary spirit because when Pathan and Briton confronted each other, each saw a Man – aware of death, deprivation, exhaustion and hardship, but above all Courage. Over the years the cruel and harsh terrain was softened by a mutual sense of respect arising from each knowing that the other admired and displayed the same qualities – first courage, then loyalty to the side you happened to be fighting for at that moment, and personal honour. The long history of nearly a hundred years of conflict between these two races resounds with pious sentiments about one fighting for his religious beliefs and the other for law and order, whereas it might just have been that both found fighting added a little spice to life! Those soldiers, probably officers, sufficiently articulate to ponder on the Pathan did not always see him in the same light: 'Ruthless, cowardly, robbery, cold-blooded, treacherous murder are to him the salt of life,' wrote one. 'Brought up from his earliest childhood amid scenes of appalling treachery, nothing can ever change him ... a shameless, cruel savage'. Another saw him differently: 'To set against his vices the Pathan is brave, sober, religious according to his lights and, on the whole, clean living; he has a ready sense of humour ... is a lover of sport

impossible for the fragmented Pathan nation to act together against the common foe. Even the holy men who always fanned the flames of war could not cement this fragile unity. When Pathans went out to battle they did so not as Pathans but as Afridis, Orakzais, Mahsuds, Mohmands or Wazirs. Characteristically, it was the most troublesome and warlike tribes that the British most admired, particularly the Pathans – the meek, subservient tribes were despised.

... And, to those who can speak and understand his queer guttural language, he is amazingly good company.' And another: 'There is a sort of charm about him, especially about the leading men, which makes one forget his treacherous nature ... For centuries he has been on our frontier at least, subject to no man. He leads a wild, free, active life in the rugged fastness of his mountains, and there is an air of masculine independence about him which is refreshing in a country like India.'

John Ayde said of them: 'They are poor but brave... and although turbulent and difficult to deal with, still have a great love of their country and cherish their independence, possessing qualities that we admire in ourselves, and which deserve consideration and respect.'

In 1855, when Britain's frequent encounters with them were getting under way, the Secretary to the Chief Commissioner of the Punjab wrote a report on the Frontier tribes: 'Now these tribes are savages – noble savages, perhaps – and not without some tincture of virtue and generosity, but still absolutely barbarians nevertheless ... They are thievish and predatory to the last degree ... They are utterly faithless to public engagements; it would never occur to their minds that an oath on the Koran was binding, if against their interests. It must be added that they are fierce and bloodthirsty ... They are perpetually at war with each other. Every tribe and section of a tribe has its internecine wars, every family its hereditary blood-feuds, and every individual his personal foes

Above left: Hayat Khan, a Nimcha tribesman, 1879.

Above: Adal, a man of Hazara, 1879.

... Reckless of the lives of others they are not sparing of their own ... They possess gallantry and courage themselves and admire such qualities in others.'

In their uninviting territory, law in the normal sense of the word could not be administered because no system of maintaining law and order could be imposed; tribes were always feuding with one another and lacked recognised chiefs so that there was no overall body with which to deal. Every tribesman was armed and skilled in the use of his weapons which he was prepared to use without compunction, so that it required the frequent intervention of British and Indian armies to capture an outlaw, force a tribe to come to terms, or punish (invariably destroy) a village.

And, of course, it was an unparalleled training ground in which every British soldier of the Queen's Army sooner or later served. Here in the appalling heat of summer and cold of winter, in rocky mountains and passes, the 19th-century British soldier could prove himself, among comrades whose respect he cherished, in unrelenting contests against foemen like himself bred for battle, with the same fierce sense of independence, customs and violent way of life, albeit on a more primitive scale.

The Pathan, tall and lean, moved with predatory grace, inner ferocity reflected by an impressive face framing hawk-like eyes, prominent hooked nose, thin cruel mouth half concealed by shaggy scrofulous beard (dyed when whitened by age). Tribesmen living in the north-east wore hair clipped short, south-western warriors had it long, ranging from carefully combed and curled bobs to greasy ringlets. The Afridi was also tall, wiry and muscular, with a long, gaunt face, high nose and cheekbones, long dark hair, but with a fair complexion; he walked with a characteristically springy stride. Beneath a large long and loose white robe (angarka) – on the Afridis it was a coarse, home-made blue garment – he wore loose tattered ankle-length white cotton trousers, sometimes taken-in at the ankle; around a pointed cap (kullah) a turban or lungi – a sash that could be worn over the shoulder as a body covering or round the waist as a cummerbund, when it also served as a repository for a large flintlock pistol, two or three long knives and a razor-sharp curved tulwar (sword); in cold weather a poshteen (sheepskin coat) worn with the hair inside, or a cloak (chadar). On bare and filthy feet he wore leather sandals (chaplis); Afridi sandals were made of grass. Resting lightly on the shoulder or cradled in the crook of the arm was a long-barrelled jezail, always loaded and ready to fire.

Although quite without any uniform characteristics except for always being unwashed and dust-covered, so assuming the colours of the rocky slopes on which they lived and fought, Pathan tribes wore clothing of varied colour and cut. Mostly white and dirty, black and dark blue were favoured by the Bunerwals in the Buner Valley area; Khyber Pass Afridis a coarse grey or blue angarka and white trousers, Wazirs a dark brick-red or dark blue turban and a dark-red or pink lungi; Orakzais preferred pearl-grey robes; while the Turis of the Kurram Valley (physically different in that they were short and compact) liked earrings and wore a dark blue angarka with white or vice versa, with a blue or white turban and cummerbund. The Shiranis, of medium height and thin, tied a black blanket around the waist and another over the shoulders, a sheepskin cloak and a turban made from white cotton cloth. Brooding in appearance and often carrying a hawk on the wrist, the Wazir's tribal dress consisted of a nat-

ural colour or white *angarka* of coarse sheep's wool, a dark-red or dark-blue *lungi*, white cotton trousers and a white *chadar*. A Wazi *malik* or head-man from Bannu was described as wearing dirty cotton robes set off by a pink *lungi* over shoulder and breast, with '... a rich shawl intertwined into locks that had never know a comb ...' and thick boots laced with thongs and rings. Pathan *malik*s also wore more ornate clothing – from the Jandol Val-

ley an Utman Khel headman affected a crimson waistcoat encrusted with gold lace over a cotton *angarka* whose flow-ing sleeves buttoned at the wrist, his loose cotton trousers buttoned above the ankles above native-style pointed-toed sandals; a richly embroidered skull-cap and ornamented sabre com-plemented his outfit.

Frontier tribesmen were superb war-riors, bred to their trade of fighting; perhaps the best marksmen in the

Above: The death of Wigram Battye of the QVO Corps of Guides, during the Second Afghan War, 1878.

world at the time, in the mid 19th century their long-barrelled *jezails* had a longer range and were more accurate than the smoothbore muskets of British and Indian infantry. At this period Indian units were sometimes armed with Brunswick rifles sighted to only 250 yards, some even had smoothbore muskets issued for use in the Peninsula and at Waterloo. Later, most tribesmen used locally produced rifles effective at 400 yards. The Afridis, made relatively wealthy through the subsidy paid them by the British to keep open the Khyber Pass, could afford to buy modern rifles so that some used Enfields and even breech-loading rifles. The *jezail*, a flint-lock firearm six feet long, was sometimes so heavy it had to be fired from a rest which gave it a range of up to half-a-mile. In later campaigns of 1896–8 many tribesmen had Martini-Henry rifles; Russian agents and unscrupulous traders sold them breech-loading rifles, sometimes condemned weapons from the Frontier stations. North-West Frontier natives have always been known as superlative manufacturers and imitators of firearms, and for much of the period the Adam Khel Afridis of the Kohat Pass were the Frontier's armourers and provided a local source of weapons, while many came in from Afghanistan. In the Tirah Campaign of 1897, when Afridis and Orakzais combined to form an army of 40–50,000 men, some tribesmen had Lee-Metford rifles captured in previous affrays, and throughout the Victorian period many of their best marksmen had more than one rifle and used loaders to speed-up their rate of fire.

British officers at the head of Indian units, conspicuous by their different headgear (sun-helmets) and their demonstrations of forthright leadership, were perfect targets for concealed marksmen; in the days before the introduction of khaki, infantry in red tunics made shooting easy for tribesmen hidden in perfect natural cover or behind stone sangars on the hillside, while the troops could see nothing whatsoever to fire at. Fortunately, the tribes had no artillery – an Afridi headman is quoted as saying: 'With the exception of your field and mountain guns – which we have not got – man to man we are as good as any of you ...' In fact, it was common knowledge that it was probably the little mule-borne mountain gun – Kipling's famous Screw-Gun – first used in 1852, that won many battles for the British. Perhaps not very accurate, but the use of artillery in the hills had a great morale effect upon the wild tribes of the Frontier, who hated it.

Other native weapons included the *tulwar*, a curved sword with scimitar-shaped blade, and a *chora* (heavy knife or mini-sword) with a blade more than 2 feet in length, a 5-inch brass-mounted bone or ivory hilt, carried in a brass-ornamented black leather sheath. Some tribes – the Chagarzais and the non-Pathan Kohistanis – carried iron-bladed spears; shields were circular, made from steel or animal hide, and had metal bosses. Horsemen carried a profusion of arms – one or two short brass-bound carbines, two or three pistols and a knife in the cummerbund, and a side-slung sword. Groups or bands of tribesmen carried flags; these might be square or triangular, in a variety of colours (red was a favourite) and devices.

Tribesmen, born hunters and mountaineers, were natural guerilla-fighters accustomed to utilising all the defensive advantages of their rugged and rock-strewn terrain, aware that the true art of fighting their defensive campaigns consisted of fighting no battle at all if it could be avoided – but remaining ever-present, ever-threatening and ever-active so as to be ready to seize any opportunity presented by Fortune or a military blunder by the opponent. Then, from an empty landscape, from behind every rock and boulder, hundreds of tribesmen would appear to threaten flanks and rear, particularly if by coming down too quickly from high ground the British had lost their advantage of 'crowning the heights'. Experienced Frontier-hand Colonel C. J. Younghusband wrote: 'Afridis may be driven all day like mountain sheep, but when night begins to fall and their tired pursuers commence of necessity to draw back to lower levels for food and rest, then this redoubtable foe rises in all his strength, and with sword and gun and huge boulder hurls himself like a demon on his retiring enemy.'

His skill lay not in winning battles but in harassing British lines of communication so that a large force had to be kept back to protect it. The tribesmen had no lines of communication to worry about, although they did not like an enemy across their lines of retreat and a show of doing this was often enough to cause a less than stouthearted tribe to pull-out of even the strongest positions. Utterly reckless of life, they could assemble their *lashkars* (tribal armies) in a few hours and disperse as quickly; carrying food, water and ammunition enough for a few days prevented supply problems and they would melt away when these were exhausted.

With the exception of the Waziris, most tribes preferred to fight defensively from a prepared position, inviting attack on their almost invisible sangars (stone breastworks made from materials at hand) or their stone or mud forts. Most villages were enclosed by mud walls surmounted by thorn-branch *chevaux-de-frise*, with towers enfilading approaches.

A deadly and effective defensive measure employed by some tribesmen was the stone-shoot, made in a place where a precipitous incline dropped on to the path beneath – ideally at some unexpected and exposed point. On the hill above, boulders were collected and, when an enemy appeared, were rained down in a continuous storm of missiles. The men operating it were usually invisible to soldiers on the path below, and the shoot was usually unturnable; in operation it was almost impassable to troops.

The Pathan would fight to the death to prevent his village and territory from invasion, as was demonstrated in 1863 at the start of the Ambela Expedition when the British marched through Bunerwal territory to reach the Hindustani Fanatics at Malka, causing all the Pathan tribes to forget their blood-feuds and other differences and pick up guns and ammunition, sling a food-bag over the shoulder, and set off for the Ambela Pass to fight the British.

Repeated demonstrations of Pathan excellence at guerrilla warfare over more than half a century aroused undisguised admiration in the British soldier; General Lockhart told British regiments severely mauled by a small Afridi *lashkar*: '... you are facing perhaps the best skirmishers and the best natural shots in the world ... the country they inhabit is the most difficult on the face of the globe ...' A noted war correspondent told his British readers: 'the Pathans ... are mountaineers of the best type. Born and bred amongst steep and rugged hills ... inured to extremes of heat and cold, and accustomed from childhood to carry arms and to be on guard against ... treacherous kinsmen ... it is small wonder that they are hardy, alert, self-reliant, and active, full of resource, keen as hawks, and cruel as leopards.'

To their guerrilla expertise the Afridis added professional knowledge of

Right: Afridi hillmen – North-West Frontier.

54

British field tactics gained during service in the Indian Army and Frontier Militia. They made good and loyal soldiers when in British service, but notoriously restless and homesick, their

terms of service were shorter than normal with the result that many trained soldiers were always available to aid their tribes against the British – this was particularly evident during the Tirah Expedition of 1897–8 when British drill manuals and musketry instructions books, translated into Urdu, were found in deserted villages. Colonel H. D. Hutchinson, correspondent of *The Times*, did not entirely agree: 'The have absolutely nothing to learn from us, these Afridis. Contra-wise. their dashing and bold attack, the skill with which they take advantage of ground, the patience with which they watch for a favourable moment, and their perfect marksmanship – all these qualities have again and again won our admiration.' All these things the Army knew well already.

In 1842, Pollock's army became the first ever to force the Khyber Pass, something that not even Tamerlaine and Akbar the Great had managed to do; on his return journey the uncrushed Ghilzais sniped at his force all the way. Conversely, 25 August 1895 was the blackest day in the British history of the North-West Frontier, when the Khyber Pass was lost – such a blow to British prestige that an unparalleled effort had to be made to recover it and punish those responsible – the Afridis and the Orakzais, the biggest threat to British rule on the Frontier. In the extensive campaigns that followed, learning a lesson from the slogging-match at Dargai, these tribes resorted to fighting in the way they knew best by attacking supply columns and survey parties, sniping at patrols, foraging parties and even the main body of the army, pressing heavily on their rear, besides cutting and removing miles of telegraph wire. Colonel C. E. Callwell wrote feelingly of these tactics: 'It is in concealing themselves, in conducting fleet movements through difficult ground, in appearing suddenly in threatening force at points where they are least suspected and in dispersing without necessarily losing tactical cohesion when they find themselves worsted, that the masters of this art (partisan warfare) single themselves out and display their warlike qualities. Such methods are bewildering to the commanders of disciplined troops opposed to them.'

In 1897, for the first time in history, the Frontier tribes were beaten to their knees. Of course they did not stay there and continued to be a repeated source of trouble until the British quit India in 1948. They were crushed in 1897 by the most calculated policy of destruction ever perpetrated by the British in India, when a great swathe of scorched earth was seared across their lands in a highly effective demonstration of what has always been British policy on the Frontier. A civil administrator put it succinctly: 'In almost all cases, the aggressive tribes behaved badly before, and well after, suffering from an expedition.' It was not, of course, designed to make the tribes love the British.

Over the years not all British leaders had agreed with it, but General Sir Neville Chamberlain – no doubt reflecting on his major campaign at Ambela in 1863, said: 'To have to carry destruction, if not desolation into the homes of some hundreds of families is the great drawback to border warfare, but with savage tribes to whom there is no right but might, and no law to govern them in their intercourse with the rest of mankind, save that which appeals to their own interests, the only course, as regards humanity as well as policy, is to make all suffer, and thereby, for their own interests, enlist the great majority on the side of peace and safety."

The purpose behind these frequent punitive expeditions, this scorched earth policy directed against crops and livestock, was to create maximum inconvenience and abject poverty to the tribe which, as a whole, was being held corporately responsible for an outrage and, not yielding to pressure and paying compensation, had to be punished. Lacking bargaining power and faced with British implacability (it could not really be otherwise, for unpunished raids would simply have led to more raids) the Pathans usually chose to fight and invariably lost. It was an imperfect and harsh policy in a harsh land, where there seemed no alternative to treating the belligerent tribesmen as fierce animals, confined in a game-reserve, to be subsidised if they stayed there to prey on their fellows, and aware that transgression meant punishment.

Winston Churchill served with the Malakand Field Force and wrote of the Pathans from first-hand knowledge: 'Every influence, every motive, that provokes the spirit of murder among men, impels these mountaineers to deeds of treachery and violence ... to the ferocity of the Zulus are added the craft of the Redskin and the marksmanship of the Boer.'

It is fitting to end discussion of perhaps the greatest irregular warriors in the world by considering those who held them in check for more than a century – young men from the pastoral peace and urban harmony of Great Britain thrust against them on nightmare terrain. It was a point of honour on the Frontier not to leave wounded men behind, as death by inches and hideous mutilation was invariably meted out to those who fell into the hands of Pathan tribesmen and their womenfolk.

8
Allied Native Units formed on the North-West Frontier of India

Right: An Afridi of the Guides Infantry.

The minor campaigns that flared-up regularly on the North-West Frontier of India ensured a more or less permanent chance of active service for the British soldier throughout the Victorian era, when at least a fifth of the British regiments in India were in the north-west at any time. Familiarising him with the sound of bullets and gunfire, it was good training for the soldier, teaching him the need to make best use of cover under conditions of persistent sniping by unseen riflemen, and acquainting him with the stresses of guards, sentry-duty and night-marches under active-service conditions. This emphasises the dividing line between experience and lack of it, when comparing newly arrived inexperienced British regiments made up of boys in their early twenties with hardened Indian frontier regiments composed of Sikhs and Gurkhas, for example. In the early part of the Victorian era it was taken for granted on the frontier that the British were the storm troops and the Indian units would be used in support. But this had changed by the time of the Mutiny in 1857, and from then on it was imperative to prevent the British regiments from looking inferior. In this they were aided by being one step ahead in their weapons, because until the Kitchener period new weapons were usually

issued to British troops first. This policy was followed partly as a heritage of the Mutiny and partly for reason of economy.

For more than half a century a picked body of native troops kept watch over the North-West Frontier territory, waging an interminable struggle against the fiercely independent tribesmen. Most of the fighting was hard and losses were considerable, but until 1897 no battle honours were awarded. Then Chitral, Tirah, the Malakand, and the Punjab Frontier had medals issued, with clasps for separate campaigns, but the regiments of the old Punjab Frontier Force, which held the border for 50 years, were never authorised to add to their colours the first two names of their old and familiar title.

At the end of the Second Sikh War in 1849, nearly a thousand miles of Punjab border had to be held, but only Peshawar was to have a garrison of regular troops, the remainder being the responsibility of the Punjab Irregular Force, eventually retitled the Punjab Frontier Force, but known to all as 'The Piffers'. Formed immediately after the subjugation of the Punjab in 1849, it was formed of men from tribes beyond the border, soldiers of the disbanded Sikh army and men of the Punjab, officered by selected captains and subalterns from the three presidencies of Bengal, Madras and Bombay. It was composed of five cavalry regiments, ten battalions of infantry, two mountain and two field batteries of artillery, and the famous Corps of Guides. The cavalry regiments each had 588 troopers, the infantry 800 riflemen; all wore the Guides' khaki uniform – white drill uniform material dyed with tea, coffee, or curry powder.

For about the first twenty years of their existence the Punjab Frontier Force was continuously engaged, bearing the brunt of every expedition on the frontier until they became the élite of the Indian forces and experts in mountain warfare. During their first half-century three of their members achieved the rank of field marshal and sixteen were awarded the Victoria Cross. From 1 August 1886, the Piffers came under the orders of the Commander-in-Chief, India.

The mainstay of the Force was the predominantly Pathan Queen's Own Corps of Guides, created in 1846 by Sir Henry Lawrence, who recognised the need for a small force of fighting men, operating outside the normal framework of the Regular Army, to guide regular units in the field and provide intelligence for their officers. To this end, it was to consist of a minimum number of European officers and a maximum number of Indians familiar with the frontier, and was raised by Lieutenant Harry Lumsden with Lieutenant William Hodson as second in command. Initially consisting of a single cavalry squadron of 109 men and three infantry companies totalling 190 men, by the early 1850s the force had expanded to about 1,000 strong and by 1857, when the Mutiny broke out, their strength was about 14,000 by which time the Guide's colours and emblem of crossed *tulwars* and the motto 'Rough and Ready' had become the mark of the frontier's corps d'élite.

Pathans made up the backbone of the Guides, mainly Yusufzais and Khattacks, although recruitment was not restricted to them; Sikhs, Gurkhas, Punjabi-Muslims and even some Hindus served in the ranks. It was known for sepoys and *sowars* to attach themselves to the Guides, without pay and even providing their own horses and weapons, so that they could be on the spot to take the place of a man who fell in action. Without exception, they perpetually relished a brisk engagement, and hardly a campaign took

Above: Sir Harry Lumsden, who raised the Corps of Guides.

their presence by wearing the usual scarlet tunics; in time, they became know as the 'Mudlarks'. As would be expected from such notable 'Frontier hands' as Lumsden and Hodson, the training given to the Guides was made as realistic as possible; although for a while their formal drill instruction was given by the 60th Royal Rifles.

Another famed frontier force, acknowledging only the Guides as their equal, were the Khyber Rifles, formed in 1879, after the Treaty of Gandamak, from inhabitants of the area, to guard the Khyber Pass from their more turbulent fellow Afridis. Originally designated the Khyber Jeza-ilchis, from the matchlock weapons they furnished for themselves until issued with service rifles, their fellow Afridis called them the Sur-Lakkais (red tails) because of the pieces of red cloth fixed to their turbans, in the manner of the proud red hackle of the Black Watch, until they were garbed like the Guides in appropriate khaki. For nearly twenty years they policed the Pass, besides fighting in two major campaigns outside their own territory.

Two formations of the Frontier Force, both named after men who had made their mark in Indian history, were Coke's Rifles (the 55th Regiment, later 13th Frontier Force Rifles) and Wilde's Rifles (the 57th Regiment, later 4th Battalion, 13th Frontier Force Rifles). Formed after the Sikh War in 1849, from disbanded Sikh soldiers, usually with one company each of Sikhs, Dogras, Pathans and Punjabi-Muslims, they were a valued element of the Punjab Irregular Force.

Perhaps the most admired and respected of all native regiments were the Gurkhas, who have always had a great affinity with British soldiers, particularly those of Highland regiments. Following two long and hard campaigns against these Nepalese hillmen in 1814–16, the Honourable East India

place in the hills without the Guides being prominently involved. A further inducement was one of the highest pay scales in the Indian Army, together with the prestige of being one of the Guides, comparable to the pride of a British Guards regiment. There was always a long waiting list, and Lumsden used the rifle-range as an entrance examination, the best marksmen being enlisted.

Lumsden clothed his Guides in uniforms made of a rough local fabric known as khaki, the loose-fitting garb being suitable for the climate and blending into the terrain over which they operated, rather than advertising

Company raised the 1st, 2nd and 3rd Regiments from their ranks, then the 4th and 5th Regiments at the time of the Mutiny; the 6th 8th and 9th were at first local levies, and the 7th and 10th plus some second battalions came into being and fought in Afghanistan under Roberts. Their battle honours included the Punjab Frontier, Malakand 1895, Tirah 1897–8, Swat, Mohmand and Kurram Valley Force 1897, and Chitral. Until the 1870s their ranks were filled by recruits from the Himalayan Districts initially overrun by the Gurkhas, so that many of them were Garhwalis; then recruiting-parties were allowed into Nepal proper, and in 1887 at the raising of the 2nd Battalion of the 3rd Gurkhas, Garhwalis were drafted into it from other battalions and their places taken by native Gurkhas. Three years later this battalion was renamed the Garhwali Regiment, continuing to wear Gurkha-type uniform and to be armed with the *kukri*.

The moral effect upon the frontier tribesmen of artillery was considerable, but the difficult country and the absence of roads made it almost impossible to deploy horse or field artillery. Since the Seven Years War battlefield mobility had become an essential aspect of field artillery and, after a variety of draught-animals had been tried on more extreme terrain, a mountain battery of 3-pounder guns carried on pack-mules was employed by Wellington in his Pyrenees Campaign of 1813 during the Peninsular War. Subsequently, a similar formation was used by the British Legion during the Carlist Wars in Northern Spain in 1836–40, and an officer of the Bengal Artillery serving in that campaign formed, in 1840, a Native Mountain Train of six 3-pounder guns with mule-transport for service in Afghanistan. This Train was disbanded in 1844 but so successful were its achievements that in 1850 the Hazara Mountain Train

Above: Thirty-four wearers of the Star 'For Valour', all serving at one time in the Corps of Guides.

came into being. This, the first of the Indian Mountain Batteries, made its debut in the Black Mountains in 1852 with 3-pounder smoothbore bronze guns, gun, trail, wheels and two pairs of ammunition boxes per gun being carried on battery mules. These weapons were not very accurate and perhaps their effect upon the tribesmen was more moral than physical, but to improve the gun by lengthening its barrel and increasing its calibre while retaining it in one piece was impossible owing to the limited carrying-capacity of the pack-mule. Eventually the problem was solved by the invention of a gun whose barrel was in two sections that screwed together; the two sections being carried one per mule. Before that, in the early days of

Right: An Afridi N.C.O. of the Khyber Rifles.

rifled Mountain Artillery, the gun in use was a one-piece 7-pounder, weighing about 200 pounds.

In 1889, Mountain Artillery became a separate branch of the Royal Regiment of Artillery, with ten batteries forming a permanent British mountain branch; at the time of the extensive frontier campaigns of the late 1890s there were eight British Mountain Batteries and eight Native Mountain Batteries with British officers. Each battery consisted of six guns, the British batteries being armed with the 2.5-inch R.M.L screw-gun, and native batteries partially with that weapon and partially with the 7-pounder R.M.L gun. The guns were carried by 138 ordnance mules, besides which there were 76 transport mules and six ponies; each mule carried a part of a gun or its carriage, with a 'relief' mule to replace any casualties and to share the load. With an average height of 13.3 hands, the mule is a very hardy animal and very sure-footed so that mountain guns can go anywhere that infantry can manage, giving them a ubiquitous quality that played a vital role in many campaigns on the frontier. Rarely a year passed without one or other of the Mountain Batteries seeing service, providing experience which bestowed upon them the reputation of being among the most practically efficient arms of the Army in India.

Throughout the second half of the 19th century local tribesmen enlisted in the Guides and other Punjab Frontier Force Regiments, or Border Military Police and locally-raised militias, attracted by the regular pay, the uniforms, the camaraderie – and the license to kill their fellow tribesmen. Forts, some of them crude crazy affairs, others impressive stone citadels ,were scattered across the hills and garrisoned by the Militia whose presence often prevented a potential tribal rising. However, this was not enough to prevent the outbreak of a holy war in 1897, aimed at driving the British from the tribal homelands. The gravest crisis since the Mutiny, it was the climax of seething resentments that had bedevilled the frontier since the end of the Sikh Wars in 1849. During that period of 48 years, as many punitive campaigns had had to be raised by the Indian Government to quell tribal defiance; in one three-year period in the 1870s, there had been ten major expeditions into tribal territory, and no part of Britain's Empire was so overripe for insurrection during the last two decades of the 19th century as India's North-West Frontier.

9
Chronology of Campaigns on the North-West Frontier of India, 1847–1900

Following the conquest of Sind in 1843 and the successful Sikh Wars of 1845–6 and 1848–9, British India found itself saddled with an ill-defined border on Central Asia, extending in a great sweep from the Mekong River and Siam in the far east, along the vast Himalayan range to the spurs of the Hindu Kush, the inhospitable Afghan hills, and the deserts of Baluchistan. Throughout the 19th century a steadfast watch had to be kept along this immense extent of frontier, on every tribe and clan, each pass and each trade-route, where every rock could conceal a foe. The 'little wars' which arose from this were the staple diet of the British and Indian Armies throughout the Victorian period, with few barren years.

In eight years from the ending of the Second Sikh War in 1849 to the Sepoy Mutiny in 1857, there were at least eight major and a dozen minor expeditions against erring Frontier tribes, many led by ubiquitous Victorian generals whose names were household words. Queen Victoria's reign as Empress of India was milestoned by innumerable such campaigns – the major operations and certainly those involving British regiments, are detailed here:

October 1847	Swat Valley	Expedition of newly formed Guides and Sikh infantry under Lawrence and Lumsden.
December 1849	Sanghao	About 2,000 men with artillery.
February 1850	Afridis	Force under Sir Colin Campbell with General Sir Charles Napier (C-in-C).
March 1852	Swat Valley	Sir Colin Campbell's force.
May 1852	Swat Valley	Sir Colin Campbell.
May 1852	Utman Khel north of Peshawar	Sir Colin Campbell
November 1853	Bori villages in Jowaki Pass	22nd Regt; Gurkhas; Guides (under Hodson) and Mountain Artillery.
August 1854	Mohmands	22nd and 42nd Foot, Native infantry; guns.
August 1857	Narinji village	27th, 70th, 87th Foot, etc. (c.2,000 men).
April 1858	Khudu Khel	General Cotton and 5,000 men.
Autumn 1863	Ambela Expedition against Hindu fanatics and Bunerwals	General Sir Neville Chamberlain Originally intended to be a 3-week promenade, this turned out to be the largest operation of the period, lasting three months

		at a cost of nearly 1,000 casualties, half the total losses sustained between 1849 and 1890 in 42 expeditions on the Frontier.
January 1864	Area Fort Shabkadar	1,800 men incl. 3rd Rifle Brigade and 7th Hussars.
January 1866	Sanghao	4,000 Native infantry and cavalry.
Summer 1867	Black Mountains	10,000 British and Native troops.
August 1867	Black Mountains	9,500 men with artillery.
October 1877	Jawaki Afridis	2,000 British and Indian troops.
February 1878	Utman Khel	Small force of Guides cavalry and infantry tribe under Battye and Cavagnari, the latter soon to be murdered in Afghanistan. Battye was killed in 1895.
March 1878	Shakot in the Swat Valley	Same force.
November 1878	Khyber Pass Afridis	2,500 British and Indian troops.
January 1879	Zakha Khel Afridis of the Bazar Valley	General Maude with 3,500 British and Indian troops.
March 1879	Opening route from Kandahar to Quetta	The Thai-Chotiali Field Force (8,700 British and Indian troops).
April 1879	Mohmands	Fighting retreat, with relief columns.
December 1879	Zaimukhts	General Tytler with 3,000 men.
January 1880	Mohmands	Dakka Column (1,000 British and Indian troops, and Landi Kotal Column 2,500 men).
October 1880	Malik Shari Wazirs	General Gordon, 1,500 British and Indian infantry and cavalry, with guns.
April 1881	Mahsud Wazirs	Two columns under Generals Kennedy and Gordon (c.6,000 British and Indian troops).
November 1881	Opening up new route into India from Kandahar	The Border Field Force.
October 1884	Zhob Valley tribesmen	General Tanner with 5,000 British and Indian infantry, cavalry and guns.
September 1888	Black Mountains	General McQueen with 9,500 British and Indian troops in the Hazara Field Force.
October 1890	Zhoh Valley Shiranis	Zhow Field Force under General G. S. White. Finding no enemy, they climbed the highest mountain in the range, to impress the natives.
January 1891	Ovakzai tribesmen and Afridis in the Khanki Valley	1st Miranzai Field Force under General Lockhart. 2nd Miranzai Field Force (General Lockhart) 7,400 British and Indian troops. Small expeditions had been sent out previously against the Ovakzais: Chamberlain in 1863, Jones and Cavagnari in 1868, Keyes in 1869.

March 1891	Black Mountains	General Elles with 7,300 British and Indian troops and 15 guns.
September 1892	Isazai tribes in Baio and Chagarzai territory	General Lockhart with 6,250 British and Indian troops. First use of Maxim guns on the Frontier.
December 1894	Mahsuds and other tribesmen of Waziristan	General Lockhart and Waziristan Field Force (3 Brigades British and Indian troops).
April 1895	Chitral tribes-men and tribes of the Malakand	Fort at Chitral besieged. Relief columns under Kelly and a force under General Low in what became a major campaign.
June 1897	Madda Khel tribe in the Tochi Valley	The Tochi Field Force (General Corrie-Bird) two Brigades British and Native infantry, cavalry, guns.
August 1897	Ovakzais and Chamkannis in the Kohat Pass	General Yeatman-Biggs and c.2,000 British and Indian troops.
July 1897	Afridis in the Malakand (Swat Valley)	A major war beginning with attacks on forts in the Malakand, then General Bindon Blood's Malakand Field Force of more than 10,000 men had several hot engagements before quelling the trouble.
August 1897	Mohmands and others attack Shab-kadar fort	Colonel Woon, then General Elles and a force from Peshawar.
August 1897	Mohmands and Koda Khel Baezai tribe	Mohmand Field Force under General Elles, later joined by Malakand Field Force (General Blood).
January 1898	Bunerwals and Chamlawals in the Tanga Pass	General Blood's Buner Field Force (two infantry brigades).
October 1897 to June 1900	Afridi and Orakzai tribes in the Tirah Valley	Tirah Expeditionary Force under General Lockhart – 44,000 British and Indian troops in one of the greatest of all the Frontier Wars.

10

Operations on the North-West Frontier of India, 1847–1900

In 1847 there began the frequent punitive expeditions of British and Native troops to bring law and order to the North-West Frontier. The militant tribesmen of the Swat Valley had long considered the plains of Peshawar to be open ground for cattle-stealing. Realising that only a show of force would change these habits, in October 1847 Major Lawrence, together with Lumsden and troops of the newly formed Corps of Guides, and some Sikhs, had a brisk action with the tribesmen before returning to British territory.

In December 1849 Lieutenant-Colonel Bradshaw led the 60th Rifles; 61st Foot; some artillery, cavalry and 200 men of the Guides under Lumsden, to attack and destroy the insurgent village of Sanghao, which had refused to submit. The village was very strong, lying beneath a precipitous rock two hundred feet high and protected on each side by spurs with steep paths up which the tribesmen retreated when the force attacked. Later, about 10,000 tribesmen from many parts of the area congregated in and around the village. Holding them frontally with artillery and infantry, the cavalry charged in from the flank in a completely successful attack that dispersed the tribesmen in all directions, leaving the village to be destroyed. British losses were 3 killed and 22 wounded.

(In January 1866, Brigadier-General Dunsford with 4,000 Native Infantry and Cavalry with artillery again destroyed Sanghao and other insurgent villages and the villagers were directed to re-establish themselves on sites away from the hills and more readily accessible to law and order.)

In February 1850 a punitive expedition set out after a large force of Afridis had attacked and almost wiped out a party of Sappers working on the Kohat Pass road. In Peshawar at the time, was the Commander-in-Chief, General Sir Charles Napier, who immediately ordered out a force under the command of Brigadier Sir Colin Campbell and accompanied it in person. Fourteen days' rations were taken and the troops were told that there were to be no reprisals and that any man found plundering would be hanged or flogged. In addition to native cavalry and infantry, the force included the 60th Rifles; the 61st Foot and the 98th Foot, with Horse Artillery including $25^{1}/_{2}$-inch mortars carried on elephants.

The village of Akhor in the Pass was defended by tribesmen on the heights around it. Ascending on the right, the 60th Rifles and 1st Punjab Infantry, commanded by Captain J. Coke, and the Guides under Lieutenant H. Lumsden, advanced on the left. The enemy, behind stone breastworks, strongly opposed the advance but the position was quickly carried by the 1st Pun- | jabis, covered by two Horse Artillery guns. This village was destroyed

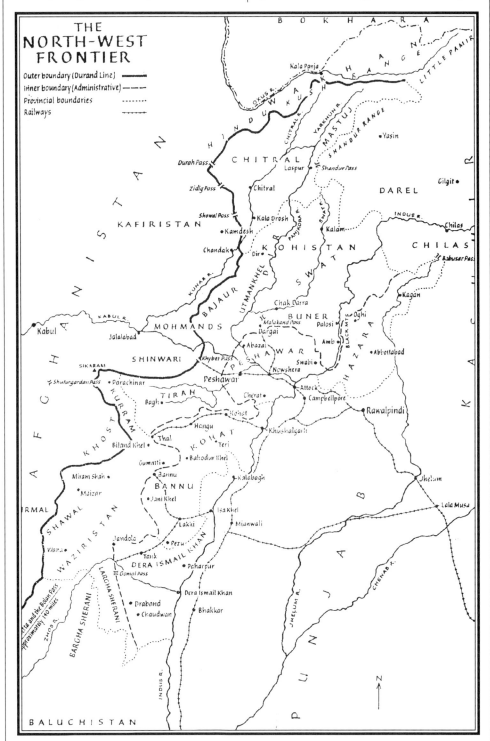

THE NORTH-WEST FRONTIER

Outer boundary (Durand Line) ———
Inner boundary (Administrative) – – –
Provincial boundaries · · · · · · ·
Railways ┼┼┼┼┼┼

together with Zargun Khel farther on, after being attacked by the 60th and 98th Regiments, assisted by the Horse Artillery. After being kept awake all night by a desultory fire on the camp, the march continued next day through the narrow and difficult Pass, commanded by tribesmen on the heights above, which had to be stormed by the 1st Punjab Infantry on the left, while a detachment of the 60th Rifles, with support of the 98th, took the heights on the right. Throughout the day, the rearguard were under constant attack by large groups of tribesmen.

During the night, a picquet of the 23rd Native Infantry beat off an attack on the heights to the front of the camp, while those to the rear were firmly held throughout the night by two companies of the 31st Native Infantry under Captain Dunmore. The party of Native Infantry sent up next morning to relieve them took the wrong path so that Dunmore's force came down before the heights were occupied, which allowed the watchful tribesmen to swarm in and badly cut-up the descending troops who had to be extricated by artillery.

After burning villages and crops, the force turned back on 13 February, having to fight their way through the narrow defile with Afridis fiercely opposing them in front and on the flanks and rear. Nineteen men were killed and 24 wounded in these operations.

On 11 March 1852, a force under Sir Colin Campbell marched into the Swat Valley to confront several thousand tribesmen in the area of Sam Ranizai. The tribesmen came to terms and without fighting offered to pay a fine, but withheld payment so that further coercion was necessary. On 15

Below: The North-West Frontier of India – The Shaturgardan.

May Campbell led forward his force of 3,270 men including the 32nd Foot; the Guides and Punjab Cavalry and Infantry; Gurkhas and other Native Infantry with horse artillery and two heavy howitzers drawn by elephants.

Elephants were as useful in this difficult and mountainous country as they were in jungle terrain, but they required considerable amounts of bulk food and had to be suitably led – each elephant required a specially trained driver (*mahout*) capable of keeping him up with the ordinary train; when guns or wagons stuck at narrow corners on steep mountain roads the elephants could push from behind with their heads. But they were dangerous under fire because they panicked, so elephant batteries had bullock teams to take the guns in and out of action under enemy fire.

In considerable strength, the tribesmen were holding a deep nullah near Shakot. Campbell planned to break the enemy's centre with artillery fire and then attack on the left with the cavalry while the infantry went forward in line of quarter columns, advancing in echelon of regiments from the right. The infantry charged home under heavy fire and the Gurkhas had a sharp hand-to-hand fight. The Horse Artillery galloped to the edge of the nullah and enfiladed the enemy whenever they could fire without hitting the British troops – during the course of this action the guns fired 2,613 rounds.

Suddenly the tribesmen broke and fled, chased by the cavalry and the Horse Artillery who repeatedly unlimbered to fire upon the fugitives so that the enemy suffered heavy losses before dispersing. The British casualties were eleven killed and 29 wounded. Shakot was destroyed and the expedition returned to British territory.

In December 1852, following the murder of officers of the Customs Department by the Hassanzai tribe, a force of Native troops including Guides with a troop of Royal Artillery with four guns and a Mountain Battery under Lieutenant-Colonel F. Mackeson went out. Although encumbered with tents, camels and the equipment needed for a normal march, the three columns successfully negotiated the snow-clad Black Mountains and its passes. In several small engagements they defeated the tribesmen and destroyed their villages at a cost of fifteen killed and wounded.

In 1852 the Utman Khel, a tribe of Pathans who occupied the hills to the north of Peshawar, constantly raided into the fertile valley below. On 11 May 1852, Colin Campbell with a force of artillery, cavalry and infantry, including the 32nd Foot, Gurkhas, Sappers and Miners and Guides Infantry, marched out and attacked the village of Pranghar on a hill flanked by spurs and heights. Musketry from the village was considerable but gradually diminished as shells from the guns burst in clouds of dust among the mud huts and towers. Then Campbell sent in the infantry who carried the village at the run, driving the tribesmen before them – after which the abandoned village was destroyed. The official account said:

'Considering that ten pieces of artillery opened on their village, it must be owned that its inhabitants made a gallant defence. But for our guns we should have sustained heavy loss – walls and flanking defences being formidable.'

The tribesmen of the Bori villages in the Jowaki Pass were a constant source of trouble by their raiding down into the Kohat and Peshawar districts. On 29 November 1853 a force including the 22nd Regiment; the Gurkhas; the Guides and Mountain Artillery set out to reach the villages by an alternative route through the Sargasha Pass which was so narrow, steep and winding that it was only possible to proceed through it in single file. Against some opposition, the villages were reached and Lieutenant Hodson led his Guides to capture the surrounding heights. The mountain guns destroyed the towers of the mud-fort defending the nearest village, and in a short time the defenders abandoned the place which was set on fire.

The 22nd Regiment and the Gurkhas, aided by artillery, drove the enemy before them and by noon heavy columns of flame and smoke were rising from every Bori village. Throughout, the tribesmen poured down matchlock fire from the surrounding hills. Pressed at every step by the tribesmen, the force now began a fighting retreat until they came to Taruni where they were concerned to find hundreds of Afridis of other tribes sitting on the hills watching the battle – they had promised their loyalty but the temptation to come down and cut off the harassed force must have been very great. Instead, they send deputations to the Bori tribesmen warning them not to come any further and actually brought water to the thirsty soldiers.

Moving out on to the plain on an easy level road, the force reached camp at 11 p.m., having been under arms for eighteen hours at a cost of 8 killed and 29 wounded from the force of 1,700. The Afridis' losses were somewhat fewer.

In August 1854 troops under command of Colonel S. J. Cotton went out to destroy some border villages of the hostile Mohmands. The force included the 22nd and 42nd Foot, together with Native Infantry, Cavalry and guns.

Shahmansur Khel, the first village, was defended both by matchlockmen in the houses and towers and by tribesmen on the heights surrounding the village. Mountain guns drove the enemy off these heights and the infantry were able to clear the village which was destroyed, the houses levelled by elephants and the grain stocks carried away or burned. By the same methods two other villages were captured and destroyed at the cost of 1 killed and 16 wounded.

1858 – 1867

In April 1858, Major-General Sir Sydney J. Cotton led an expedition of 4,877 men, including the 31st and the 90th Foot, with six guns in operations against the Khudu Khels. Operating in three columns, the force destroyed forts, villages and crops, driving the enemy from their positions by bayonet charges after highly effective fire from the Enfield rifles which were being used for the first time on the Frontier. The enemy closely harried the force on the return journey after operations costing 6 killed and 29 wounded.

On 2 January 1864 some 6,000 Mohmand tribesmen threatened Fort Shabkadar, garrisoned by about 1,800 men with three guns commanded by Colonel N. Macdonell and including 150 sabres of the 7th Hussars and 3rd Battalion, The Rifle Brigade. The tribesmen advanced, shouting and screaming, in an irregular crescent formation to be attacked by the 7th Hussars who gradually folded the enemy's right on his centre while the artillery raked their retiring wing, causing considerable casualties. Charging three times, the Hussars continued the turning movement until the tribesmen were driven away by the Rifle Brigade, advancing in skirmishing order. British losses were 2 killed and 17 wounded.

In 1867 disturbances with the Black Mountain tribes made it necessary to mount a punitive expedition which, to save weakening the border posts, was supplied from stations in the Punjab and the North-West Provinces. To reach the scene of operations, many

Above: Pari Durrah, the entrance to the Jugdulluk Defile, Khyber.

regiments marched long distances during the hot season – the 38th Foot covered 250 miles in ten days; the 20th Punjab Native Infantry marched 422 miles and the Sappers and Miners 600 miles in twenty-nine days of forced-marches. During their march the 6th Foot lost 38 men from heat apoplexy. Under the command of Brigadier-General A. T. Wilde, the force, including the 6th, 19th and 38th Foot with Guides Cavalry, Gurkhas, Sikhs, Punjabi Infantry and Bengal Cavalry with artillery, numbered 9,500 men. Lasting three weeks, the arduous operations in mountainous country, constantly hampered by lack of water, saw strong defensive positions stormed and rebellious tribesmen completely defeated for the loss of 5 men killed and 29 wounded.

THE AMBELA EXPEDITION, 1863

In the face of objections from Sir Hugh Rose, the Commander-in-Chief, it was proposed in autumn 1863, to send a punitive force about 5,000 strong through the Chamla Valley to drive out into the plains beyond a fanatical group of Pathans who had been raiding from their village at Malka. No trouble was expected from the other tribes in the territories bordering the Chamla Valley who had no sympathy for the fanatics and held different opinions. Sir Neville Chamberlain, a soldier of great experience and reputation, commanded the force which included the 71st Regiment, the 101st Regiment, Native Infantry Regiments, Guides, Cavalry and Infantry and Mountain artillery.

The force left on 18 October, intending to move northwards through the Ambela Pass during the first day's march, so as to be about sixteen miles down the Chamla Valley on the second day; the third day's march of six miles would bring them to Malka. In the event, the force found great difficulty in traversing the Ambela Pass and after three days the elephants and baggage animals had blocked the Pass and the entire expedition had ground to a halt.

The Bunerwals, tribesmen who lived in the area alongside the Pass, were afraid that the British operations were merely a cloak to annex their territory, so they were closely watching the operations. The enforced three day halt in the Pass appeared to confirm their fears and the alarmed Bunerwals attacked the column, wrecking in a single stroke the original British plan because an advance up the Chamla Valley with a strong and warlike tribe flanking the line of march for seventeen miles was out of the question.

With one man in ten of his force sick, Chamberlain found himself in serious trouble as other tribes flocked to join the Bunerwals. Although his camp was fortified with stone-walled forts on each flank, broken ground made it easy for the enemy to creep up to the defences. On 25 October their attack was only repulsed after several hours of hard fighting, costing the British force 124 men killed and wounded.

Unable to advance into the Valley that lay before him because of his inability to keep the Pass open behind him, Chamberlain could not move from his present position into open ground for that would mean giving up the Pass and retaking it at serious cost every time he wished to send out a convoy. He had no choice but to sit and await the reinforcements marching long distances to reach him.

The key to Chamberlain's defences was the Crag, a high rocky hill commanding all the lower defences but only large enough to be defended by twelve men. On 30 October, it was captured by the tribesmen who were driven out by the bayonet in a day of constant attack and counter-attack which cost 55 casualties. On 6 December a party working on the road into the Chamla Valley were cut off by tribesmen and lost 3 British officers and 78 other ranks in fighting their way back to the main force. On 11 November, in a night attack on the Crag, which lasted for six hours, 2,000 tribesmen attacking in waves were beaten off with the bayonet and sometimes with rocks and stones. It was 48 hours before the small garrison, their muskets so foul that they could scarcely load them, were able to be withdrawn and replaced by a fresh party. On the 13th, distracted by a flanking fire and then shaken by a sur-

prise attack, the small garrison panicked and rushed down the slope. Immediately the 101st Regiment retook the position at a cost of 158 men.

On 18 November the British lost another 118 men in fighting that lasted from morning until dark. On the 20th, in fighting that lasted from nine in the morning until mid-afternoon, the garrison of the Crag were again thrown out but Chamberlain turned his guns upon the position to prevent the enemy occupying it, and then personally led the 71st Regiment and the 5th Gurkhas in a counter-attack. The Crag was recaptured, but Chamberlain himself was severely wounded, in addition to 137 men killed and wounded.

The morale of the British force was low after a month on the defensive against a wily and dangerous enemy in his own hills where he could always concentrate superior numbers. The weather was growing steadily colder and there were more than 450 sick and wounded who could only be sent to the rear with strong escorts which seriously weakened the defensive strength of the force. Fearing a repetition of the disaster at Kabul in 1841, it was decided that the force should be withdrawn but Chamberlain refused, so Sir Hugh Rose sent Colonel John Hyde and Major Frederick Roberts, V.C., to the Ambela Pass to report on the actual state of affairs. At the same time he directed substantial reinforcements to force-march to the area. Hyde and Roberts justified Chamberlain's optimism, formed the opinion that the attack on 20 November had seriously weakened the tribesmen and advised Sir Hugh Rose that operations should be prosecuted to the bitter end.

On 30 November, Major-General Garvock took over from the wounded Chamberlain, to command a force strengthened to about 9,000 men, including the 93rd Highlanders. The force pushed forward and in two days' hard fighting lost 24 men killed and 157 wounded while causing the tribesmen to disperse to their homes.

For prestige reasons, it was imperative that the village of Malka, the original objective of the expedition, should be destroyed, but in the time it would take to organise an expedition large enough to do this, the enemy would be able to reorganise. So, banking on the hope that the tribesmen had no stomach left for fighting, it was decided to send some British officers with a small escort to destroy Malka. It was a gamble that might cost the lives of every officer and man of the party. On 19 December Colonel Reynell Taylor, Major Roberts and four other officers with an escort of 200 Guides, set out from Ambela and burned Malka on the 22nd. They returned slowly, surrounded by thousands of threatening tribesmen who repeatedly halted the small column while they argued whether it should be massacred or allowed to proceed. The accidental firing of even a single shot would have precipitated a massacre, but the tribesmen allowed the force to near Ambela and then withdrew to their own territory.

Originally intended to be a promenade lasting three weeks, the Ambela Expedition had lasted three months at a cost of nearly 1,000 casualties, half the total losses sustained between 1849 and 1890 in 42 expeditions on the North-West Frontier, making it the largest operation of that period.

OPERATIONS AGAINST THE KHYBER PASS AFRIDIS, 1878

From the moment the British Army advanced into Afghanistan in November 1878, the Afridis of the Khyber Pass began to give trouble. Against them Brigadier-General G. A. Tytler, V. C. led a force of about 2,500 infantry and cavalry with five guns, including the 1/5th Fusiliers and the 51st King's Own Light Infantry, with Sikhs, Gurkhas, Punjabis and Bengal Lancers. After marching through the deserted

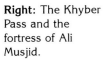

Right: The Khyber Pass and the fortress of Ali Musjid.

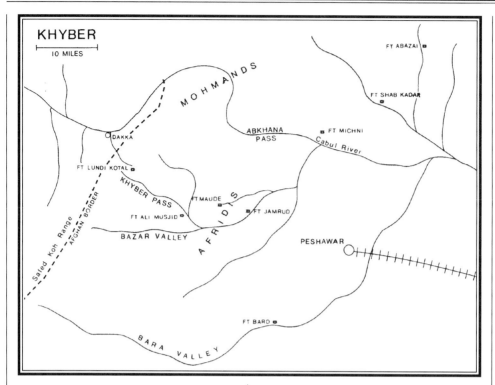

Bazar Valley, on the night of 21 December the force encamped and during the night they became aware that the tribesmen were all around them. Next morning the force marched up the steep, winding road to a pass that ascended 1,000 feet in 1½ miles. The troops came under fire immediately they began their march, and had to charge the enemy at the head of the pass before the column of men, horses, baggage and guns could get on. Throughout, the rearguard were fighting fiercely and only kept the enemy back with considerable difficulty.

Near the top of the pass the road narrowed to a rocky defile only five feet wide; about 200 yards from its exit was a sheltered position occupied by about 100 tribesmen who had crept unobserved through a narrow gorge. Emerging, the head of the column, ranks broken, was met with a hail of fire. The tribesmen were dislodged by rifle fire and the bayonet which allowed the column to move on to open ground four miles from the top of the pass where the tribesmen ceased to oppose them. Astonishingly only one man was killed and seven wounded. The expedition carried out their tasks and returned to British territory.

OPERATIONS AGAINST THE JOWAKI AFRIDIS, NOVEMBER 1877 TO JANUARY 1878

In October 1877 a punitive expedition against the Afridis was mounted. Under Brigadier-General Keyes, it consisted of 2,000 troops of the Punjab Frontier Force; the 5th Gurkhas; a small number of cavalry and six guns, operating with a force from Peshawar under Brigadier-General Ross which included the 51st Foot, the 9th Foot, 4th Battalion The Rifle Brigade and Royal Horse Artillery, and native infantry.

Advancing steadily under fire through narrow passes and defiles, the force destroyed villages and crops and blew up some fortified towers. At 3 a.m.

on 1 December the troops, with mule batteries, clambered over a succession of ridges to take the Jowakis' principal stronghold of Jummu completely by surprise, so that the Jowakis fled to the hills. The British lost nine men.

Towards the end of January 1878 the Jowaki headmen sought peace but found British conditions unacceptable; then, after 250 British cavalry had attacked and completely defeated them on 15 February, they came in and submitted. During the campaign British losses were 11 killed and 51 wounded.

EXPEDITION AGAINST THE UTMAN KHEL, 1878

Typical of the skirmishes and small affrays that flickered constantly on the wild North-West Frontier of India was that against the Utman Khel, made more notable because the officers concerned figure prominently in later events. In February 1878 a small force of Guides Cavalry and Infantry mounted on ponies, under the command of Captain W. Battye with Captain P. L. N. Cavagnari, made a night ride of 32 miles, dismounted and marched a further two miles over heavy ground and then four miles along a river bank and climbed for a mile up a steep narrow path to reach the village of Sapir at daylight. Before the sleeping tribesmen knew what was happening, the troops rushed in and took the village.

In March 1878, the same two leaders led another small expedition to Shakot in the Swat Valley when, using the same tactics as before, the village was surrounded after a night march and the villagers surrendered without resistance. The force then marched back to Mardan, covering 50 miles in twenty-four hours.

THE THAL–CHOTIALI FIELD FORCE, 1879

In March 1879 troops moving back to India from Kandahar were to open up

Right: The Fort of Khelat-i-Ghilzai, 95 miles from Kandahar.

a direct route from the Punjab to Quetta and Pishin so as to avoid the length and heat of the Sind–Bolan route. The force included the 15th Hussars, 70th Regiment, Gurkhas, native cavalry and infantry with mountain guns, making a total of about 8,700 men.

Only slight opposition from tribesmen was encountered and repelled causing 200 enemy casualties after accurate shelling by the mountain guns followed by a charge. British losses were 3 killed and 7 wounded.

OPERATIONS AGAINST THE MOHMANDS, 1879

In April 1879 a small detachment of 130 native troops under Captain Creagh were besieged in the village graveyard of Kam Dakka by tribesmen who were encouraged by the fact that the force had no artillery. From early morning until mid-afternoon several assaults were only repelled by bayonet charges and towards the end of the day, with ammunition running low, the enemy were within 60 to 100 yards.

In the late afternoon three companies of British Infantry, two guns of a mountain battery and two companies of Gurkhas and a troop of Bengal Lancers arrived from Dakka. Withdrawal without heavy loss was impossible until the enemy could be dislodged from strong positions within one hundred yards of the graveyard. The Bengal Lancers managed to advance under cover to a point within 200 yards of the enemy and then charged and dispersed them down a steep bank into the river. The besieged left the graveyard, carrying their dead and wounded and, as soon as the tribesmen flooded into the enclosure, the mountain guns shelled it with common-shell and percussion fuzes.

The withdrawal was led by the cavalry and infantry with baggage and wounded following, then the mountain guns with detachments of infantry and cavalry in the rear. Throughout, the enemy pressed the rearguard closely and kept up a heavy fire upon the column.

Next morning the hard-pressed column was met by a force from Dakka and the tribesmen dispersed, having lost about 200 killed and wounded. The British casualties were 6 killed and 18 wounded; Captain Creagh was awarded the Victoria Cross.

EXPEDITION AGAINST ZAKHA KHEL AFRIDIS OF THE BAZAR VALLEY, 1879

Failing to tender their submission in January 1879, a force was assembled to destroy the tribe's villages in the Bazar Valley. Lieutenant-General Maude commanded a force of about 3,500 infantry and cavalry with eight guns (two of them on elephants). In three columns, the force included the 5th Fusiliers, 25th Foot, 51st Foot, 1st/17th Foot, 4th Battalion The Rifle Brigade and Royal Artillery, besides Gurkhas, Guides and other native troops. The columns marched for some days over difficult country and frequent skirmishes occurred while the columns were sniped incessantly by day and night. Feeling that a further advance might well spark off a frontier war, General Maude halted in a strong defensive position and sent back for instructions. Although given permission to advance, the force returned to British territory, having lost 5 killed and 13 wounded.

EXPEDITION AGAINST THE ZAIMUKHTS, 1879

This tribe of Pathans began to give trouble during the war in Afghanistan and on 8 December 1879, Major-General Tytler, V. C. moved out with the 2nd/8th Regiment, 85th Foot; Royal Artillery, Native Cavalry and Infantry.

Below: The storming of Afridi sangars in the Bazar Valley, 1879.

Marching on the stronghold of Zawo, the troops advanced by a ravine and, greatly aided by the screw-guns, the right-hand column got on to high ground and hotly engaged the enemy while the main force pushed on up the rough bed of the narrow defile until they arrived at a village about $3^{1}/_{2}$ miles from their objective. The two guns of the mountain battery worked round to the left of the ravine and opened fire at 700 yards' range while the 29th and 85th in two columns attacked the village and captured it.

Attacking again at 7.30 a.m., they dispersed the tribesmen from new positions then, pushing on up the defile, fought off attacks from both sides with the guns covering the infantry who were advancing under heavy fire and showers of boulders from the heights. Zawo was captured and burned together with two other villages and fortified towers. The British force lost two men killed and two wounded; 40 tribesmen were killed and 100 wounded.

THE EXPEDITION AGAINST THE MOHMANDS, 1880

Taking advantage of the British Army's being occupied in Afghanistan, the Mohmands rebelled and on 11 January 1880 crossed the river into British territory. On the 14th a column was sent out from Dakka to attack the Mohmand position frontally while another column from Landi Kotal

attacked them in flank and rear – with the river in their rear and attacked on all sides the enemy's destruction was almost certain. The Dakka column consisted of 94 sabres of the 6th Dragoon Guards; 110 men of the 1st/25th King's Own Scottish Borderers; Bengal Cavalry and 600 Native Infantry with four guns and Horse Artillery, under the command of Colonel Boisragon.

On the morning of 15 January the force was drawn up facing the Gara heights where the Mohmands had built strong breastworks and entrenchments. After an hour and a half's shelling by the artillery, the tribesmen were driven from their entrenchments and dispersed when the infantry were sent in to advance steadily up the rugged precipitous hillside covered by the fire of the guns. By midday, the utterly routed tribesmen were fleeing down the reverse slopes.

The Landi Kotal column, consisting of 5th Fusiliers, 25th (King's Own Scottish Borderers) with native cavalry and infantry and guns, had to make their way in single file along a very narrow path, so precipitous that some mountain battery mules went tumbling over the edge. It was repeatedly necessary to send forward skirmishing parties to occupy heights that commanded the route, and at one stage a 1,000-foot hill had to be cleared by a storming party of infantry. It was not until 5 o'clock in the afternoon that the troops arrived within range of the river bank along which the enemy were fleeing, and although the mountain guns opened up at 1,000 yards' range the enemy made good their escape and crossed the river.

Because of the late arrival of this column the combined operation was a failure, but the Mohmands had suffered a severe defeat, losing 70 killed and 140 wounded. The British losses were two killed and three wounded. The Horse Artillery fired 200 shells and the infantry 14,000 rounds in this operation.

EXPEDITION AGAINST THE MALIK SHAHI WAZIR SETTLEMENTS, 1880

A force under Brigadier-General J. J. H. Gordon, consisting of 250 men of the 85th Regiment (King's Shropshire Light Infantry) with 250 native cavalry and the same number of native infantry with two Royal Artillery guns, went out to extract fines levied against this tribe for cattle-stealing. Knowing that the expedition had to traverse the length of the Kabul Khel settlements to reach the Malik Shahi settlements, the tribe felt secure because they would have sufficient warning to enable them to escape to the western hill country. To avoid this, on the night of 27 October 1880, the force marched from Thal, making a wide detour so that they arrived at their intended positions by daybreak and the villagers awoke to find themselves surrounded. The force confiscated 2,000 head of cattle and these together with 109 prisoners were taken back to Thal. On the 30th the tribal chiefs came in and made their submissions and paid their fines, and the prisoners were released.

EXPEDITION AGAINST THE MAHSUD WAZIRS, 1881

With the end of the Afghan campaign, troops were available to deal with the Mahsud Wazirs who had been concerned in several serious outrages on the Thal–Kurram Road. Two columns were assembled and moved out in April 1881. From Tank, the first column was under Brigadier-General T. J. Kennedy and consisted of 4,000 Native Infantry, Cavalry and Artillery of the Punjab Frontier Force. The second column under Brigadier-General J. J. H. Gordon, was formed at Bannu and included the 4th Battalion The Rifle Brigade, Native

Infantry, Cavalry and mountain artillery with Royal Artillery guns. The two columns were accompanied by about 9,000 camp-followers, more than 4,000 mules, 1,500 ponies and 6,500 camels.

Keeping in touch by heliograph, the two columns advanced through the Wazir country against very little resistance. Most of the inhabitants of the area had never seen a European and their attitude was naively friendly. The expedition broke up on 22 May, having sustained 32 casualties while proving to the Mahsuds that no natural difficulties of their country could protect them from punishment.

In November and December 1881, the Bozdar Field Force, which included the Manchester Regiment, marched back to India from Kandahar and, striking off north-east through unknown country, opened up a new route. There was considerable sickness among the troops because of the general unhealthiness of the area at this time of year.

THE ZHOB VALLEY EXPEDITION, 1884

The depredations of the aggressive tribesmen of this region made a settled frontier impossible, and work on roads and railways could only be done sporadically. To warn off the tribesmen, an expedition was ordered into the Zhob Valley in October 1884. Under Brigadier-General Sir O. V. Tanner, it included 1st Battalion Worcestershire Regiment; 2nd Battalion North Staffordshires and 1st Battalion North Lancashires; native infantry and cavalry made up the remainder of the force which totalled 4,220 infantry, 561 cavalry and ten guns. Only scattered resistance and sniping was encountered, and after marching 700 miles the force was withdrawn on 22 November. There were no casualties, but considerable sickness among the troops, again because of the general unhealthiness of the area during this season.

THE HAZARA FIELD FORCE, 1888

On 7 September 1888, a punitive expedition under Brigadier-General J. W. McQueen was sent into the Black Mountains to punish tribes for killing two British officers and four Gurkhas. Totalling nearly 9,500 officers and men, the expedition consisted of three Mountain Batteries; one Company of Sappers and Miners; nine Battalions of Native Infantry; Royal Irish Regiment; Northumberland Fusiliers; Suffolks; Seaforth Highlanders and Royal Sussex, plus Gatling guns. No tents were taken and the only baggage allowed was half a mule-load for each officer and 16 pounds per man for the other ranks. Each man carried 70 rounds of ammunition with 30 rounds per rifle loaded on mules; rations for five days were carried.

Marching out in five columns on 3 October 1888, the troops were fiercely engaged almost at once in rocky and mountainous country and over steep slopes and crags. The paths were so steep that even the mules had difficulty getting up them – fourteen of them went over the edge. One mile-long ascent took a column twelve hours to cover. Constant casualties were caused by tribesmen sniping the camps during the night. Many villages were destroyed during hard and bitter fighting before the tribesmen submitted and were dispersed. British casualties consisted of two officers and 23 men killed, 3 officers and 54 men wounded. The columns were back in British territory on 13 October.

OPERATIONS IN THE BLACK MOUNTAINS, 1891

On 18 March 1891 Major-General W. L. Elles marched out with a force of

7,300 officers and men with fifteen guns; included were Seaforth Highlanders, Royal Welsh Fusiliers, and K.R.R.C. Operating in two columns, the troops were heavily engaged in the narrow streets of Kanar village where the enemy fired from the flat rooftops. After the force had occupied all the commanding ground within range, the tribesmen were forced to withdraw; those tribes that did not make their submission had their villages burned. The British force had returned by 9 June, having lost 9 killed and 39 wounded.

EXPEDITION TO THE ZHOH VALLEY, 1890

Major-General Sir George White led the Zhoh Field Force into the Zhoh Valley on 1 October 1890 to capture a rebel leader, Dost Muhammad, but, unable to find him or his band of outlaws, there was no fighting. Subsequently, General White decided to impress the natives by marching his troops to the top of the celebrated Takht-i-Suliman, the highest part of the great mountain range, taking paths up the precipitous eastern face that were considered impassable even to mountain cattle and sheep. Often scrambling up on hands and knees after lying sleepless under 6° of frost at night, the men accomplished the hard climb. In his dispatch, General White wrote, 'The ascent ... was by far the most difficult physical operation I have ever called upon soldiers to perform, and the fact that the British soldiers and Baluchi sepoys, fully accoutred, scaled these dangerous heights, will not be lost on the Shiranis.'

THE MIRANZAI FIELD FORCE, 1891

Although not such fine men nor as formidable as the Afridis, the Ovakzai tribe were wiry mountaineers who had frequently been troublesome so that punitive expeditions of native troops had been sent against them in the past. Brigadier Neville Chamberlain in 1863; Major Jones and Lieutenant P. Cavagnari in 1868; and in 1869 two companies of the 36th Foot took part in an expedition under Lieutenant-Colonel Keyes. The first Miranzai Field Force under General Sir William Lockhart went out in January 1891, encountering light opposition but sustaining 33 cases of frostbite because of the 20° below freezing night temperature. After an apparently successful operation the force broke up, but a few days later further murderous and treacherous attacks were made on small parties of troops. Lockhart raised another force of about 7,400 men including the King's Royal Rifles and half a battalion of the Manchester Regiment, and marched out on 17 April 1891. Covering a lot of ground, the operations were highly successful and culminated in the blowing-up of their defensive towers in the presence of tribal gatherings. The territory of two powerful tribes was traversed and mapped for the first time, and the Afridis in the Khanki Valley were shown that the British had the power to reach them. Total British casualties from 4 April to 15 May amounted to 28 killed and 73 wounded.

EXPEDITION AGAINST THE ISAZAI TRIBES, 1892

In 1892 there was a widespread coalition against the British by the tribes in the Chagarzai territory. Almost without precedent on this border, the situation could be compared to the Ambela outbreak of 1863 and, similarly due to a misunderstanding, the unrest was stimulated by the belief that a British force was going to march through Chagarzai territory to Thakot. Consequently, Major-General Sir William Lockhart mounted an expedition, consisting of 6,250 men and two guns, which marched out in September 1892 to confront the Isazai tribes in Baio. Reaching the village without any opposition, the force destroyed the fort and then withdrew. The expedition is chiefly notable for the first recorded use of the Maxim machine-gun on the frontier. Also exceptional was the unusually indifferent health record of the force; 24 men were lost to cholera.

THE SIEGE AND RELIEF OF CHITRAL, 1895

In March 1895 about 370 native troops, under Doctor Robertson, the British Agent, were besieged by large numbers of frontier tribesmen in the small stone fort of Chitral. A relief expedition of 15,000 men under General Robert Low was assembled to relieve Chitral through the Swat Valley. The force consisted of men from The Buffs, Bedfordshire Regiment, King's Own Scottish Borderers, East Lancashire Regiment, King's Royal Rifle Corps, Seaforth Highlanders, Gordon Highlanders, with Indian cavalry and infantry plus two mountain batteries. By 3 April, this force had reached the Malakand Pass and were attempting to force it.

Not knowing when the larger expeditionary force would advance to the relief of Chitral, Lieutenant-Colonel J. G. Kelly, already in the area of operations, set out for Chitral with a small force of about 500 Native Infantry and two mountain guns. They left Gupis on 28 March carrying only the barest necessities and with only enough sunglasses for a small proportion of the force so that practically everyone suffered from painful snow-blindness. The mules carrying the guns and stores found the going very hard, and half-tamed yaks requisitioned from villagers were not much better. After ten days of incredible hardships over wild and precipitous country thick with snow, the

guns and ammunition having to be either carried on poles or towed on improvised sledges by men suffering from both snow-blindness and frost-bite, Kelly's troops had their first engagement with the enemy on 9 April. The tribesmen were in a very strong position extending across the narrow Chakalwat Valley, and their defensive sangars had to be put out of action by the mountain guns whose gunners were so handicapped by snow-blindness as to be unable to lay the guns properly. Every shell had to count because it had only been possible to bring up a very small quantity of ammunition, so the guns, under very heavy fire, had to be brought up to within 400 yards of the sangars. Excellent co-operation between artillery and infantry turned the enemy out of their strong position and Kelly's men were able to manhandle their guns across the fast-flowing river and move down to Mastuj. Here they relieved Lieutenant Moberly and some native infantry who had been besieged in a small stone fort, where Kelly's force rested for two or three days until they received information by runner of the action fought by Low at the Malakand. Kelly reckoned that if they hurried they could still arrive at Chitral before the larger force got there.

The siege of Chitral fort had been proceeding throughout this time, marked by a resolute and aggressive resistance by the small defending force. The stone fort, only 80 feet square and with walls 8 feet thick, had been vigorously attacked by the tribesmen who had even run a mine to within a few feet of the walls, covering the sound of digging by playing native bagpipes and tom-toms. A sortie from the fort, about 100 strong, attacked the mining party with the bayonet and blew up the mine at a cost of 8 killed and 13 wounded, while some 60 tribesmen were left for dead in the crater.

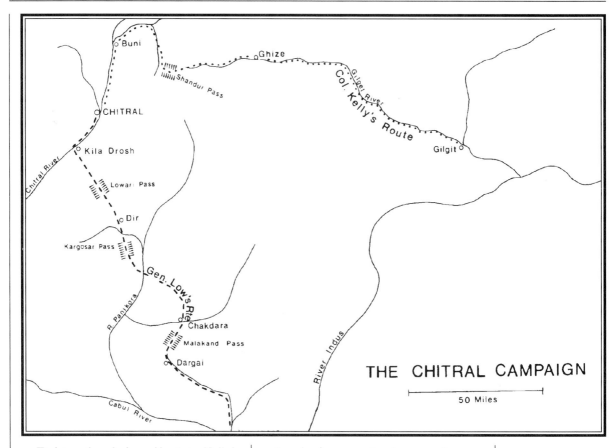

THE CHITRAL CAMPAIGN

50 Miles

Eight miles below Mastuj, Kelly's small force came upon a large number of enemy tribesmen well positioned in one of the most famous natural defensive positions in the country, reputed to be impregnable. Again, the little mountain guns did sterling work in destroying enemy sangars before Kelly's men finally put the enemy to rout after an attack which necessitated descending ravines by improvised rope ladders and climbing steep and slippery goat tracks.

Then followed five days of skirmishing in the rock-strewn defiles in front of Chitral until, on the night of 18 April, the besiegers quietly stole away and on the 20th Colonel Kelly's column marched into the fort. The siege had lasted 46 days and one-fifth of the garrison had been killed or wounded.

Low's force arrived some four or five days later after a great deal of very heavy fighting beginning on 3 April when the mountain guns shelled the enemy positions along the crests bordering the Malakand Pass (the lowest of them was 3,000 feet above the valley). Then Sikhs and Guides carried the sangars on the left and worked their way along the crest to turn the enemy's flank, being nineteen hours under arms and losing many officers who were distinguishable from their men by wearing helmets instead of turbans. The Scottish Borderers and the Gordon Highlanders worked up the centre of the Pass with the King's Royal Rifles, the Bedfords and native infantry in support. After a precipitous climb, where the men had to haul one another up, the village on the summit was carried

Right: Machine gun detachment, King's Own Scottish Borderers, Chitral Relief Expedition, 1896/7.

with the bayonet and left in flames, and the enemy were driven across the ridge into the Swat Valley beyond. British casualties amounted to 8 officers and 61 men, while it was estimated that the enemy had numbered about 12,000 men and had taken 5,000 casualties.

Next day the advancing troops encountered enemy on a high ridge. The guns came into action as the infantry advanced under fire from the heights and repeatedly attacked by large parties of tribesmen. Two companies of the Bedfords were attacked by vastly superior numbers, but magazine fire at short range halted them in their tracks and sent the survivors scurrying for cover. Although operating over most unsuitable terrain, the Guides Cavalry distinguished them-

selves here against the tribesmen who would face magazine-rifle fire but did not like lances.

The Swat River had to be crossed under fire from a ridge of hills that dominated the only ford. The Sappers attempting to bridge the river were forced to withdraw, but the Maxim gun of the King's Own Scottish Borderers and the mountain guns did good work against enemy positions on the ridge. Finally the Sikhs and Borderers were committed while the Bengal Lancers and the Guides crossed the fast-flowing river under heavy fire. Once the Lancers had reached the far bank they dispersed the stoutly resisting enemy with the lance. The Scottish Borderers, linked arm-in-arm, forded the Swat higher up and, covered by the mountain guns, carried a small fort, while

Right: Maxim guns on the march, the Chitral Relief Expedition 1897/8.

the Sikhs crossed in like fashion lower down and occupied two villages. This arm-linking method of river crossing was only possible because the troops were armed with breech-loading rifles whose cartridge cases were of brass; in the old days of paper cartridges the musket and pouch had to be held above water. British casualties at the crossing were few, given that the opposition numbered some 4,500 men who suffered heavy losses.

On 12 April Colonel Battye and his Guides passed over the Panjkora River to form a covering force on the right bank, but before daybreak the river, swollen with melted snow, rose suddenly and the bridge was swept away by logs sent down by the tribesmen. The Guides were ordered to march to a crossing two miles down-stream, but, owing to a misunderstanding, they marched out of sight and could not be covered by the fire from the left bank. Dividing his force into three, Battye retired slowly down the river bank, himself remaining with the last party to cover the retreat until he was mortally wounded. The Guides, unable to cross the river that day, made a fortified camp on the river bank and spent a long night surrounded by at least 2,000 of the enemy who were discouraged from attacking by star-shells fired across the river and the presence of some Sikhs and a Maxim gun that had been floated across the river on a raft of inflated animal skins. At daybreak the tribesmen retired leaving about 500 bodies behind; the Guides lost two officers and three men killed and 22 wounded.

Although there was constant skirmishing, no further major engagements took place as the infantry, cavalry and guns cleared the hills and slowly advanced towards Chitral. On 18 April General Gatacre, with The Buffs, Gurkhas, half a mountain battery, two Maxims and 20 days' sup-plies, was sent forward to make a dash for Chitral. But Gatacre's force were ordered not to press forward when, on the 21st, came news that the fort had been relieved by Colonel Kelly. Securing his communications as he marched, General Low steadily advanced and a few days later entered Chitral.

THE MALAKAND FIELD FORCE, 1897

In July 1897 some 20,000 Afridi tribesmen suddenly attacked the Malakand Post. Beaten off with heavy losses after several days' hard fighting, the tribesmen then turned to the Chakdara Post which survived several assaults before water and ammunition became scarce. Under General Sir Bindon Blood, the Malakand Field Force of 6,800 infantry, 700 cavalry and 24 guns, included the 1st Bn., West Kent Regiment; 1st Battalion East Kent Regiment (The Buffs); Royal Artillery and Native Infantry and Cavalry units. On reaching the Malakand camp General Blood sent out a column which successfully relived Chakdara after hard fighting.

Reinforced by 1st Battalion Gordon Highlanders, 2nd Battalion Highland Light Infantry, Punjab and Gurkha Infantry, General Blood began his advance from Thanza on 17 August, and encountered the enemy at Landaki where 5,000 tribesmen holding a long flat-top spur enclosing the valley like a great rampart were kept occupied in front while Meiklejohn's Brigade climbed the hills to threaten the enemy's left flank. The surprised and out-manoeuvred tribesmen fled from the spur pursued by cavalry. It was here that in a misunderstanding two British officers were killed; two V.C.s were awarded, one of them to Viscount Fincastle who was with the party as War Correspondent of *The Times*.

As the Swat Valley quietened, tribal risings occurred in rapid succession on other parts of the frontier.

THE TOCHI FIELD FORCE, 1897

In June 1897 the Madda Khel tribe launched a treacherous attack on a Political Officer and his escort of 300 native infantry and two guns. With only sixteen rounds per gun, the artillery came into action at 100 yards' range as the fighting retreat on foot began. Four white officers were wounded, two mortally, but all continued to lead their men as the small force retired by successive units while the guns, out of shell, fired blanks to deter the enemy. Reinforcements arrived and the tribesmen withdrew leaving a number of casualties behind. Total casualties of the British force were two officers and 21 men killed and 28 wounded.

Subsequently the Tochi Field Force was formed, a punitive expedition

Above: General Sir Bindon Blood, commander of the Malakand Field Force.

Right: The relief of Chakdara by the Malakand Field Force. Colonel Goldney with the 38th Sikhs taking a hill commanding the descent to the Swat Valley.

85

Above: The main street, Datta Khel, the Tochi Valley area.

under the command of Major-General Corrie-Bird, consisting of two brigades and including Argyll and Sutherland Highlanders and the Rifle Brigade in addition to native infantry and cavalry. Marching out on 20 July, the force engaged in sporadic skirmishing until October when the tribes submitted and paid their fines. The Tochi Field Force was gradually broken up by January 1898, having lost six men killed and eight wounded in a campaign remarkable for the unusual amount of sickness among the troops. The climate of the Tochi Valley is at all times trying and the hurried marches in the middle of the hot weather encouraged a severe epidemic of dysentery.

OPERATIONS AGAINST THE OVAKZAIS AND CHAMKANNIS, 1897

There had been smouldering discontent among these tribes since 1891 when the British had occupied the Samana Posts, and in August 1897 the situation became serious enough to warrant the sending of reinforcements to the area, among them the Royal Scots Fusiliers. On 27 August Major-General Yeatman-Biggs marched out with a force composed of 180 Scots Fusiliers, 487 Punjab Infantry with artillery and a squadron of Punjab cavalry. In an engagement that took place in intense heat, 86 of the Scots had to be carried back to Kohat in ambulances, prostrate with heat, while the total casualties were two killed and one officer and seven men wounded.

Reinforcements arrived at Kohat on the following day, including 2nd Royal Irish Regiment and a Field Battery of the Royal Artillery, and the force relieved some British-garrisoned forts with difficulty. For the next few days large numbers of tribesmen burned, raided and destroyed Posts and villages and besieged many of the forts that dotted the area, where the small British garrisons held out against large numbers of tribesmen until relief columns broke through. The operations concluded when the advancing British columns pushed back the tribesmen until the various tribes, one by one, made their submissions.

THE ATTACK ON THE SHABKADAR FORT BY MOHMANDS AND OTHER TRIBESMEN, AUGUST 1897

On the afternoon of 7 August 1897, about 4–5,000 followers of the Madda

Mullah attacked the Shabkadar Fort and looted and burned the village of Shankargarh. The attack on the fort was easily repelled by the garrison of one native officer and 46 Border Police, and at dawn next day the enemy withdrew. Later a column under Lieutenant-Colonel Woon arrived from Peshawar. It included two companies of the Somerset Light Infantry, Native Infantry, two squadrons of Bengal Lancers and four guns of the Royal Artillery.

Next morning the force advanced and found the enemy occupying a strong position on the undulating plateau at the foot of some hills. Because of the unfavourable terrain, the artillery did not open fire until an hour later than planned, and this allowed the enemy to make a determined attempt to turn the British left flank. Colonel Woon was compelled to order a retreat to avoid being cut off from the Dakka Fort on which he was based. Brigadier-General Elles, commander of the troops in Peshawar, arrived and assumed command of the force, re-organising the infantry and artillery dispositions and sending cavalry to swoop down on the enemy's left rear, immediately putting the tribesmen to flight. It was estimated that the tribesmen lost more than 200 dead and a large number of wounded; British casualties were nine dead, four officers and 61 men wounded.

THE MOHMAND EXPEDITION, 1897

In August 1897 an expedition was mounted to punish the Mohmands and to prevent any violation of Dir territory which might imperil the safety of the Chitral road. The Mohmand Field Force under Brigadier-General Elles consisted of two brigades, including the Somerset Light Infantry and Oxfordshire and Buckinghamshire Light Infantry, Native Infantry, Bengal Lancers, mountain artillery and a Maxim gun detachment of the Devonshire Regiment.

After a long and unopposed march in conditions of intense heat, the force met General Sir Bindon Blood's Malakand Field Force on 22 September and the two combined to take the Bedmanai Pass, thought to be strongly held. However opposition was not very heavy and the force lost only one man killed and three wounded. On 24 September all the villages and towers in the Mitzai Valley and the Suran Valley were destroyed. Next day in another action, involving the Somerset Light Infantry and Gurkhas, fortified villages in the Shindarra gorge were destroyed at a cost of two men killed and seventeen wounded. On 27 September, a column moved against nine fortified villages occupied by the Koda Khel Baezai tribe. In the action that followed the Oxfordshire and Buckinghamshire Light Infantry and the Gurkhas played a prominent part in dispersing the enemy, while the Sappers and Pioneers demolished the towers and forts.

The march continued slowly because the tracks were difficult and required a considerable amount of road making work, but by 4 October all the offending tribes had paid their fines and submitted so the object of the expedition had been accomplished.

EXPEDITION AGAINST THE BUNERWALS AND CHAMLAWALS, 1898

In 1897, when the general uprising of Pathan tribes on the North-West Frontier of India was quelled, only the Bunerwals and the Chamlawals refused to submit. Accordingly, in January 1898, under the command of General Sir Bindon Blood, the Buner

Field Force was formed, consisting of two infantry brigades and including the Royal West Kents, Buffs (East Kents), Highland Light Infantry, Native Infantry, Bengal Lancers, Guides Cavalry, field artillery and mountain batteries. It was estimated that the enemy totalled 3–4,000 tribesmen.

In an attack on the Tanga Pass, the artillery opened fire at 2,200 yards' range, covering The Buffs as they made a difficult climb to a ridge from where they began volley-firing at 1,500 yards' range. The remainder of the infantry made a frontal attack up steep slopes against tribesmen positioned behind stone sangars, making steady progress in the face of matchlock fire and avalanches of rocks rolled down upon them. Fast becoming demoralised by artillery fire and long-range volleys from The Buffs, the tribesmen took to their heels when the attacking infantry neared the top of the slope. Only one man was killed, but the tribesmen lost at least 50. Meanwhile, the cavalry had forced the Pusai Pass in an operation made extremely difficult by the rough track, ice and hoarfrost, and after three nights' bivouacking without baggage. Finding the cavalry and infantry in their midst the tribesmen submitted.

THE OPERATIONS OF THE TIRAH EXPEDITIONARY FORCE, 1897-8

The general object of this expedition was to exact reparation for the unprovoked aggression of the Afridi and Orakzai tribes by invading Tirah, their summer home, which had never before been entered by a British force. In difficult and largely unknown mountain territory, the force had to be prepared to confront tens of thousands of well-armed and warlike tribesmen – the Afridis alone were believed to be able to put 30,000 men into the field, at least half armed with modern rifles.

In October 1897 a force of 44,000 men under the command of Lieutenant-General Sir William Lockhart assembled at Kohat. In addition to fourteen battalions of Native Infantry and mountain artillery, the force included the Royal Scots Fusiliers; King's Own Scottish Borderers; Dorsetshire Regiment; Sherwood Foresters; Northamptonshire Regiment; Derbyshire Regiment and Gordon Highlanders. The Punjab was scoured for transport animals and 60,000 camels, mules, bullocks and carts, ponies, pack-bullocks and donkeys were assembled.

Lockhart's main column was to invade Tirah from Kohat via the Sampagha and Arhanga Passes while two subsidiary columns from Peshawar were to act in support. Before the main column moved off it was necessary to make the road fit for their transport which meant that tribesmen had to be dislodged from the village of Dargai and the ridges around it from where they could fire upon the road-parties. Dargai itself, 6,000 feet high, was only approachable over its last half-mile by climbing sheer, broken and shelving cliffs by a narrow track with an entrance on the far side of a completely exposed area of ground. The tribesmen were not holding the position in great strength, and British infantry and Gurkhas swarmed up the steep ascent and took the position at a cost of only two killed and thirteen wounded. During mid-afternoon the position was abandoned because of supply and water difficulties. The enemy closely pressed the rearguard and were only held off by mountain guns. In what turned out to be a difficult operation 1 officer and 7 men were killed, 5 officers and 29 men wounded.

Leaving Kohat on 20 October, the main force had to retake Dargai

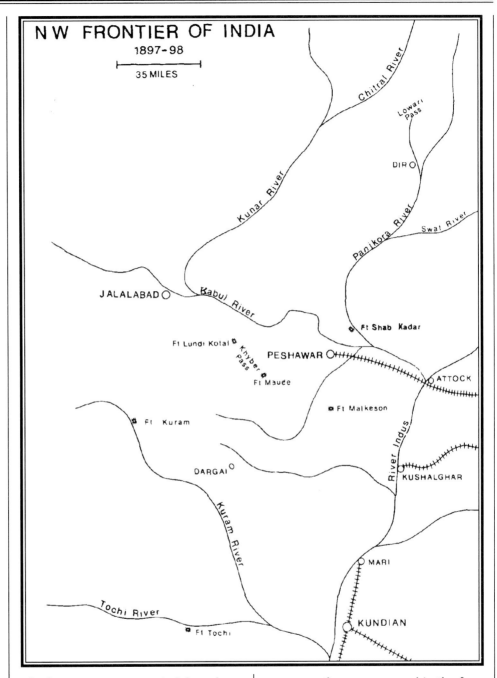

NW FRONTIER OF INDIA
1897-98
35 MILES

which was now occupied by about 12,000 tribesmen. Covered by long-range fire from the Gordon Highlanders, the Maxim gun detachment and mountain batteries, the Gurkhas formed up under cover about 500 yards from the cliff and then burst out on to the open ground in the face of an extremely accurate and rapid fire. Reaching broken ground about 100 yards on, after losing 3 officers and 50 men, they were pinned down by heavy fire. The Dorsets and the Derbyshires were put in to try to rush

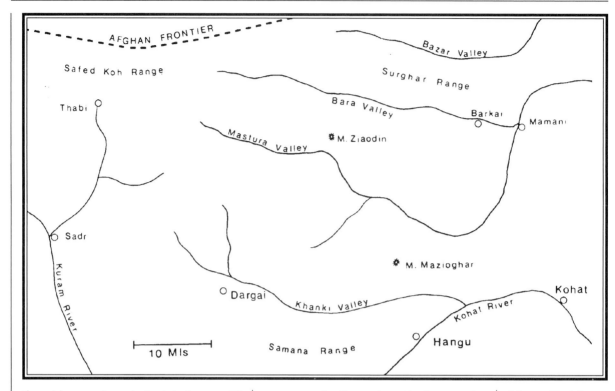

the ridge and each lost between 40 and 50 men without succeeding. The Gordons and the 3rd Sikhs were ordered up. After the artillery had maintained a rapid concentrated fire for three minutes, the Gordons dashed across the open ground followed by the Sikhs and all the other troops on the position. They swarmed up the steep slope so decisively that the enemy did not wait for the final assault but fled in all directions harried by long-range volleys. Five Victoria Crosses were awarded for the Dargai action in which British casualties amounted to 4 officers and 34 men killed, 14 officers and 147 men wounded.

On 29 October the Queen's Regiment and the King's Own Scottish Borderers stormed a ridge to take the Sampagha Pass, and on the 31st the Arhanga Pass was captured against little opposition. Throughout the advance foraging parties and baggage were constantly under attack – on the 25th one man was killed and 36 wounded when a foraging party was attacked. On 1 November in a night attack on a convoy, the tribesmen captured thirteen boxes of ammunition and the Queen's Regiment's treasure chest, besides inflicting losses. On 9 November, the Northamptons lost heavily while retiring from destroying enemy villages when they lost touch with supporting Sikhs while carrying wounded down craggy cliffs. Trapped in a nullah under heavy fire, they were extricated by Sikhs and Gurkhas with total losses of two officers and eighteen men killed, four officers and 44 men wounded. Sikhs and two companies of the Dorsets, who remained out in the darkness collecting stragglers, were cut off by Afridis and only managed to fight off the tribesmen at the bayonet point by capturing some partly burned houses and making a stand. The Dorsets were overwhelmed

Above: Sketch map of the Tirah Campaign, 1897/8.

90

Right: The Northamptons retiring down the nullah after the attack on Saran Sar during the Tirah Expedition.

and lost their officers, the survivors being brought into camp by the senior sergeant. Total casualties in this affair were four officers and 25 men killed; 6 officers and 38 men wounded. On 22 November, a column which included the King's Own Scottish Borderers and the Yorkshire Regiment went out to explore the approaches to the Bara Valley and, in returning, their rearguard became heavily engaged and lost 1 officer and 4 men killed, 2 officers and 28 men wounded.

Because of the cold weather, the troops were now obliged to evacuate the Tirah Valley, and the 3rd and 4th Brigades under Brigadier-General Westmacott, coming down the Shaloba defile to Dwa Toi in the Bara Valley, experienced some of the heaviest rearguard fighting ever encountered in an Indian frontier campaign. Progress was slow as the roads were deep in mud, and, on the morning of 11 December, a thick mist allowed the Afridis to get in close and pour in a heavy fire on the crowded and helpless transport animals and followers. Trying to get off the track, the transport became bogged down in the fields and nullahs. The enemy attacked the rearguard with great boldness and fighting continued throughout the day. Casualties became so numerous that the fighting line was seriously weakened by troops having to carry the wounded men because the *dhoolie*-bearers were too terror-stricken to perform their duty. There was no water supply at that night's camp after a day when more than 70 men had become casualties during a relatively short march. The tribesmen only ceased their attacks on the struggling force next day when the Peshawar force was encountered some four miles from Sawaikot.

On 29 January Lockhart sent out columns to capture the Afridis' sheep in the hope of bringing the tribesmen to terms. The task was carried out without opposition except to 4th Brigade from Mamanai which had to fight one of the hardest actions of the campaign. Composed of 600 men of the Yorkshire Light Infantry and the 36th Sikhs, with two guns, the force advanced through a pass, occupying the heights on each side as they moved forward. Through a misunderstanding, the native troops evacuated the heights on the west of the pass which were immediately occupied by tribesmen who poured a heavy fire into the troops below. Two companies of the Yorkshire Light Infantry sent to retake the heights were beaten back, losing officers and sustaining heavy casualties. With great difficulty the rest of the Yorkshire Light Infantry managed to cover the withdrawal until they were met at the mouth of the pass by a force sent out from camp. Owing to the hilly ground and the nature of the operation it was impossible to bring out the dead, but rifles and ammunition were saved. Total casualties were 5 officers and 28 men killed, 3 officers and 34 men wounded. This was virtually the last fight of the campaign; the Afridis tendered their submission and by the end of June only a single brigade remained in the Khyber Pass. In 1900 regular troops were withdrawn and the Pass was handed back to the care of the Khyber Rifles.

PART THREE
THE GREAT GAME: EGYPTIAN VERSION

A Highlander in the Egyptian positions at the Battle of Tel-el Kebir, 1882.

11
Britain and Egypt

Throughout the Victorian Era, when British politicians and statesmen could get their minds off India, they shared the view that Egypt was of vital importance as a link in the lifeline to India, lying across the route to that country, besides being the key to Africa, where Britain had substantial colonial possessions. Among others, both Lord Cromer, appointed British Agent and Consul-General in Egypt in 1883, and Prime Minister Lord Salisbury had doubts about the Ottoman Empire's ability to deter Russian ambitions in the eastern Mediterranean, both believing that Britain's role was to maintain Egypt as a safe and practical imperial highway to India. At that time, the only Power likely to contemplate invading Egypt was France, as the growing strength of Bismarck's Germany was still confined to Europe, and Russia was playing in the other game, beyond Afghanistan. So, when claiming to prevent anarchy in Egypt and uphold the authority of the Khedive, by landing British troops on Egyptian soil in 1882, Britain was predominantly ensuring that France did not do so first, and maintaining Egypt as a stepping-stone on the road to India. After quelling the rebellion of Arabi Pasha in 1882, British troops remained in Egypt for 74 years, during which time the country was under varying degrees of British political control.

On first entering Egypt, the British found that defeating Arabi was but the beginning; in the following year they had to consider the threat posed to southern Egypt by the rising Mahdi Mohammad Ahmed, 1,000 miles south in the Sudan. Under the nominal suzerainty of the Ottoman Empire, Egypt had ruled in the Sudan since 1820, but were now threatened with the loss of Khartoum and the Sudan, following a series of overwhelming defeats of Egyptian armies and garrisons by the militant followers of the Mahdi. If this occurred, Egypt would be defenceless. The British were thus forced into becoming the protectors of Egypt, and faced with the likelihood of having to put an army into the Sudan to quell the Mahdi. This was completely unacceptable and, following the withdrawal of a succession of ineffectual Egyptian governors from Khartoum, Britain's General 'Chinese' Gordon – who had previously held an official post in the Sudan – was appointed to Khartoum to relieve the garrisons and, with complete control of the territory, carry out a planned withdrawal. The events that followed are well known, and the problem was not truly resolved until 1898 at Omdurman – that was the end, but the beginning was a Near-Eastern adjunct

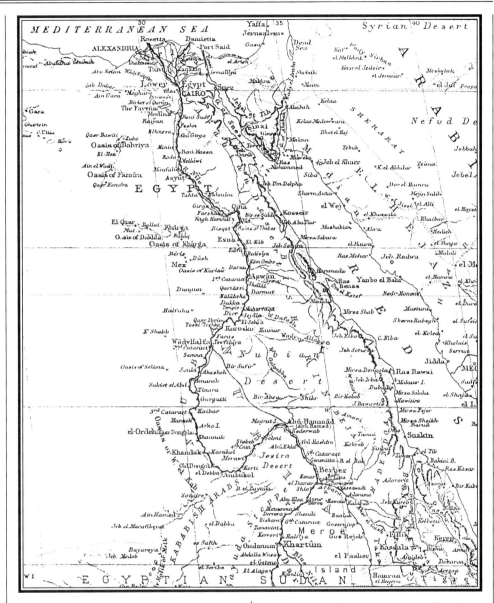

to the Central Asian 'Great Game', the prize in both cases being India. Despite this common factor, they made strange bed-fellows – the arid Sudan and the awesome crags of the Frontier of India, their respective inhabitants having totally different styles of fighting, but sharing the quality of being implacably ferocious warriors.

On these differing terrains, against such notable foes, battles transcended others of the period and, of all the campaigns fought during this long period, these two intermittent and prolonged wars best exemplify the incredibly varied nature of the campaigns the long-suffering British soldier was sent to fight. Yet, without fail they come to the forefront of the mind as archetypal Victorian colonial campaigns whenever considering the host of diverse encounters tackled by the red- and khaki-coated Victorian Army.

12
Chronology of the War with the Egyptians, 1882

1879, 26 June: Tewfik becomes Khedive of Egypt

1881, 1 February: Egyptian Army Mutiny

9 September: Palace confrontation between Khedive and Arabi; Ministers resign office.

1882, January: Arabi appointed Minister for War

March: Arabi is made a Pasha

April: Circassian officers, plotting to kill Arabi, are arrested and tried; court-martialled, their punishments drastically reduced by the Khedive

5 May: French propose that six British and six French warships be sent to Alexandria

15: The combined fleet leaves Suda in Crete

20: The fleet arrive at Alexandria; the Ministry resigns *en bloc* in protest against foreign interference

21: Arabi Pasha holds a demonstration, demanding to be reinstated as Minister of War

26/27: Egyptian troops threaten to storm Alexandria, and attack Europeans

28: Arabi Pasha becomes virtual dictator; orders Alexandria's forts to be put in state of defensive readiness, despite contrary orders from Khedive and British Admiral

11 June: Massacre of Europeans in Alexandria

7 July: Admiral Seymour threatens bombardment if defensive work is not halted

10: 24-hour ultimatum sent by Admiral Seymour; last Europeans leave Alexandria; French withdraw their warships

11: British fleet bombards forts at Alexandria

12: Egyptian troops and Bedouins sack Alexandria

13: City on Fire; Arabi and his forces withdraw outside city

14: Naval landing-parties go ashore and rescue Khedive who had been threatened by armed soldiers

15: Sailors and Marines go through city suppressing marauders

17: *Tamar* (carrying Royal Marines), *Agincourt* and *Northumberland* arrive, carrying 38th Regiment and 3/60th Rifles; General Sir Archibald Alison arrives from England and takes command of this force

22: Discovers Arabi's force entrenched at Kafrdowar; first skirmishes occur

23: *Malabar* arrives carrying 46th Regiment and a wing of 38th; these join Alison's force and move out to occupy Ramleh

24: Contact made with Arabi and the two forces face each other, within artillery range, in hastily fortified positions

25: In Britain, The Army Reserve is called out

30: Guards leave Britain

2 August: General Sir Garnet Wolseley leaves Britain

3: Marines from the fleet occupy Suez

5: A reconnaissance-in-force, including armoured train, moves over area Ramleh–Kafrdowar; engages and defeats enemy force at Mahalla Junction

6: General Graham takes command of British position at Ramleh

8: Troops from India arrive at Suez, others and units from Britain continue to arrive during next two weeks

10: Duke of Connaught, with chief-of-staff Sir John Adye, arrive at Alexandria

12: Brigade of Guards arrive at Alexandria

15: Sir Garnet Wolseley arrives at Alexandria; two infantry divisions, plus cavalry, artillery and Staff Corps, leave Britain; Mounted Infantry, under Captain Parr, carry out reconnaissance towards enemy positions; minor engagement ensues

16: Sir Garnet Wolseley, Sir Evelyn Wood and Sir Edward Hamley, accompanied by the Duke of Connaught and other generals, inspect British positions, and view Arabi's formidable entrenchments

17: Orders issued for troops to prepare to embark; units of 1st Division that had landed, re-embark

18: Work of embarkation continues

19: Ships sail from Alexandria for Ismailia; considerable enemy activity, with firing, in front of British position at Ramleh

20: Sir Evelyn Wood sends 49th Regiment out on a reconnaissance; Port Said occupied

21: Hamley sends out 42nd Regiment on a reconnaissance towards Kafrdowar; Fleet off Ismailia, embarkation begins; last of British Expeditionary Force lands at Alexandria; Sir Garnet Wolseley and Admiral Seymour at Ismailia; Nefiche occupied by General Graham; General McPherson, commanding Indian Contingent, with his Staff, arrives at Suez

22: Graham takes a strong force towards Ramses, El Magfar and Mahuta; engages enemy throughout day

23: Opposed advance continues

25: General advance against Mahuta begins; found to be deserted. Drury Lowe, with cavalry, makes wide circuit and takes Mahsameh; force encamps at both places

26: General Graham takes and occupies Kassassin

27: Mahmoud Pasha Fehmy, Arabi's Chief-of-Staff, falls into British hands

28: The Battle of Kassassin; infantry of the Indian Division, with artillery and commissariat corps, landing at Ismailia from now until 31st

29: Orders received at Alexandria for the Highland Brigade, under General Alison, and Sir Edward Hamley and Staff, to embark for Ismailia; Sir Evelyn Wood remains in charge of the city and lines at Ramleh

30: The force embarks; sails on 31st, arriving Port Said 1 September; lying in transports off Ismailia until 9 September, lands and marches to Kassassin, arriving 13 September

5 September: War Office in London issue orders for dispatch of 4,000 more troops from Britain

6: Egyptian force reconnoitres British positions at Kassassin

7: Indian cavalry and Mounted Infantry make close reconnaissance of Egyptian lines at Tel-el-Kebir; General Willis and Staff, General Drury Lowe and the cavalry arrive at Kassassin; Guards on their way there

8: Strong British reconnaissance made on south bank of Canal and desert area

9: Arabi personally present at strong Egyptian reconnaissance of British positions at Kassassin; Egyptian attack on Kassassin beaten-off

11/12: Sir Garnet Wolseley and other senior officers reconnoitre both sides of enemy's position; 87th Regiment and Pontoon Train arrive in camp

13: Battle of Tel-el-Kebir; defeated Arabi flees to Cairo; Indian Cavalry and Household Cavalry take-up pursuit of fleeing Egyptian army, arriving at Belbeis in evening

14: This cavalry force arrives in early evening, at Abbassiah Barracks outside Cairo; city and garrison surrender; Egyptians at Kafrdowar make overtures for the surrender of the position

15: Finding Lines at Kafrdowar abandoned, British from Ramleh take possession; via the re-established telegraphic communication system, Arabi and his officers offer submission to the Khedive, who refuses to accept them; Sir Garnet Wolseley enters Cairo

17: Sir Evelyn Wood and Staff enter Lines of Kafrdowar; Arabi Pasha a prisoner in Cairo

18: Egyptian garrisons of the Aboukir Forts march to Kafrdowar and surrender; Egyptian force at Tantah surrenders to the Seaforth Highlanders

20: The Khedive, escorted by Bengal Lancers, drives through Alexandria

25: Khedive leaves for Cairo

27: A Special Commission appointed, by decree of the Khedive, to consider all acts performed by civil and military persons during the rebellion; Arabi and his followers to be court-martialled

30: Great Review and March Past of British troops in Cairo

2 October: Valentine Baker Pasha arrives in Cairo from Constantinople; has audience with Khedive concerning re-organisation of Egyptian Army

5: Arabi Pasha and Toulba Pasha handed over to Egyptian Government, brought before court and charged with treason

20: Horse Guards arrive home, at West India Docks

21: March through streets to Albany Barracks; Life Guards arrive home and march through City on following day; Royal Marines land at Portsmouth; 400 officers and men receive from the Queen at Windsor the Egypt Medal announced in a General Order on 17 October 1882

18 November: Great Review of troops marching through London before the Queen.

Left: The military clearing the streets of Alexandria, Sunday 11 June 1882.

13
The War in Egypt, 1882

In 1882 Arabi Pasha set himself up as virtual dictator of Egypt, supported by many of his countrymen who flocked to his banner by his impassioned demands that the foreigner be driven from the country. As a major power, Britain found this wholly unacceptable and, in June of that year, found herself fighting for the Khedive against his own Minister of War. Claiming descent from Husseyn, the youngest grandson of the Prophet Mahomed, Sayed Ahmad Bey Arabi – Arabi Pasha – leader of the Egyptian Nationalist Party, was 48 years old when he found himself confronting the guns of the British fleet sent to Alexandria to overawe him. Entering the army as a private, he had risen rapidly to the rank of lieutenant-colonel and, having been reinstated after being cashiered on a false charge, he became the most popular soldier in the army. In 1881, at the head of the Cairo garrison, he marched to the Abdin Palace, secured the fall of Riaz Pasha, a prominent politician, and obtained a pay-rise for the army, sub-

sequently becoming Under Secretary for War in the Egyptian Government and being created a Pasha. Having declared support for the powerless Khedive, Britain sent Admiral Sir Beauchamp Seymour's Mediterranean Fleet to lie off Alexandria for some weeks, but lacked authority to land and stop the rioting and massacre of Christians in the city. Growing bolder, Arabi Pasha (known to the British sailors and soldiers as 'Horrible Pasha') set his engineers and their plentiful labour forces to strengthen the forts around the harbour and throw up substantial earthworks, besides mounting heavy guns. A Naval Officer correspondent of *The Illustrated London News* wrote:

'A few days ago Egyptian troops were exercised at shelter-trench making ... and now a very creditable series of earthworks protects their guns, some originally pointing landwards now command the harbour. Probably not far short of 150 guns of all kinds might now be brought into play against a hostile fleet.'

On 10 July 1882 the British presented an ultimatum for the surrender of the forts, otherwise they would be bombarded from the sea; on rejection, the fleet cleared decks for action. It consisted of eight battleships mounting 60- and 80-ton guns, and eleven small gunboats armed with 64-pounder and 7-inch rifled guns, besides Gatlings mounted in their fore-tops. Against them, the forts were plentifully equipped with 18- and 12-ton guns and many smaller calibre weapons. Fire was opened at 7 a.m. on the 11th and continued throughout the morning. The defences were quickly obscured by clouds of smoke and dust and occasionally magazines were set off with a shattering roar. Onlookers reported that it seemed scarcely possible for men to stand by their guns under such fire as was poured on them, admiring this unexpected obstinacy of the gunners in remaining so long at their posts, serv-

ing the guns so gallantly while the batteries crumbled about them. The Egyptian artillerymen revealed courage and determination equal to that which might be displayed by any

Above: Egyptian troops at gun-drill in one of the Alexandria harbour forts.

Left: The bombardment of Alexandria by the British Fleet.

army in Europe, their officers setting a fine example by springing upon the parapets in most exposed positions, selecting targets and directing fire. Alas, the technical ability of Arabi's gunners was unworthy of the officers who led them so gallantly, and the British fleet had only 10 men killed and 27 wounded, although 1 ship received 27 hits. By one o'clock all fire from the forts had ceased and no resistance was offered to a landing-party which spiked guns and burst the barrels of those guns not put out of action by the bombardment. An Egyptian officer of the garrison later said that about 900 were killed and wounded of the 8,000 men who manned the forts. In the city rioting, murder and incendiarism raged unchecked for two days until permission was received for a force of sailors and marines to be landed. These fought a street-by-street, house-by-house battle with the looters until peace was restored.

Far from subduing Arabi, the defeat spurred him to greater resistance so a force under Sir Garnet Wolseley was sent to destroy him; gathered from Britain, India and the Mediterranean garrisons of Cyprus, Gibraltar and Malta, by mid-August 40,000 men were lying in transports in Alexandria Bay. Deluding Arabi that the bulk of the force were going to land at that place and seek battle at the fortified lines of Kafrdowar, Wolseley landed a feint force, while the convoy sailed eastwards to disembark on 20 August at Ismailia at the mouth of the Suez Canal. General Graham took 2,000 men and a few guns into the heart of the desert to secure the precious water of the Sweetwater Canal at Kassassin. At this time Arabi Pasha had about 60,000 fighting-men disposed at the likeliest places all over the Delta – in the neighbourhood of Alexandria, at Cairo, and at Tel-el-Kebir, a commanding point on the railway between

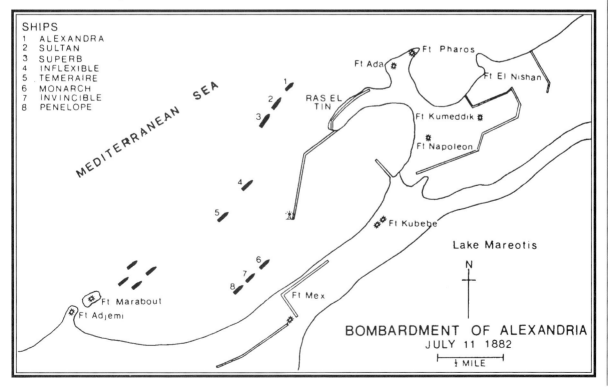

SHIPS
1 ALEXANDRA
2 SULTAN
3 SUPERB
4 INFLEXIBLE
5 TEMERAIRE
6 MONARCH
7 INVINCIBLE
8 PENELOPE

BOMBARDMENT OF ALEXANDRIA
JULY 11 1882

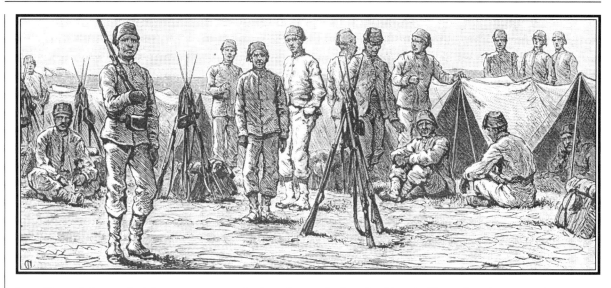

Ismailia and the capital. It was an army composed of different races and ethnic groups – Negroes of the Sudan, Arabs of various tribes, and large numbers of Bedouin tribesmen; a fairly high proportion were ordinary peasants or *fellahin*, forcibly conscripted by Arabi. A war-correspondent of *The Globe* wrote that, at Mahuta, many dead were to be seen wearing the brown felt head-covering of the peasant, and numerous woven palm-leaf baskets used to carry provisions were found. Wolseley did not consider it a formidable army, but feared that Arabi might arouse Mohammedan fanaticism to a pitch that could transform the scale and scope of the struggle.

The Egyptian military system was adapted to secure maximum strength in wartime, or minimum when the army was on a peacetime footing; every soldier passing through the ranks could be recalled, and a large proportion of the male population could be mustered if needed. Raids were made on villages for levies of fresh men, who received arms and ammunition, but no uniform and little training; whole companies being summarily drafted from one battalion to another if suspected of disloyalty. At

the time of the Arabi rebellion the army was weaker than at any period in its history, its strength being only six regiments of infantry (9,000 men); two regiments of cavalry (1,000); one regiment of field artillery (600); one regiment of coastal artillery (700), totalling in all only 11,300 men, but all old soldiers. Large numbers of veterans must have been recalled to the

Above: Egyptian infantry, 1882.

Below: Bedouins firing at the gallop.

Above: Egyptian soldiers guarding the streets of Alexandria.

Colours and numerous *fellahin* dragged from their homes and formed into regiments that could have had little cohesion or confidence in one another.

The rebel Egyptian infantry wore tunics and trousers of course white cotton cloth; tunics had a low round-fronted standing collar, six buttons in a single row, with badges and buckles all of brass bearing the star and crescent. Loose trousers and white canvas gaiters worn over black leather shoes, all equipment was black leather including straps on field-pack, which was brown or black and had a cooking-pot strapped to it, and a grey blanket-roll wrapped round it, or slung over the left shoulder and around the body. A brass-hilted, wavy-bladed sword bayonet was carried on the left side in a brass-mounted steel scabbard; the small red fez (*tarboosh*) had a short black tassel hanging from its top. Officers wore a very dark-blue, single-breasted short thigh-length tunic, with voluminous skirts and a row of eight yellow metal buttons; with it was worn a white shirt and black stock. On the shoulders were gold-fringed epaulettes, varying to indicate rank. Trousers, the same colour as the tunic, were full and tapered towards the ankles. Headgear was a red *tarboosh* with long black tassel hanging from the crown. Black leather waist belt, with square yellow metal buckle bearing star and crescent; swords were either steel, three-bar hilted in plain steel scabbard, or white hilted Mameluke-type in black leather and yellow metal scabbard. Cavalry were dressed as infantry, with black boots without spurs, instead of gaiters.

Infantry were armed with the Remington 11mm (.433in) Rolling-Block rifle, capable of seventeen shots a minute; made in the USA under contract, 60,000 had been delivered in 1876. It was also supplied as a carbine for cavalry and a musketoon for artillery; the sword-bayonet was mounted on the right side of the barrel. Because it held sand and led to 'hang-ups' of locks and breech mechanism, oil was never used on Remington rifles, which were so polished by their owners as to look as though made of silver. Their musketry left much to be desired and was always better at long rather than short range; at Tel-el-Kebir, eighteen infantry battalions, advantageously posted, poured out a hail of fire, but killed only two men! Conscripts were armed with old brass-mounted, muzzle-loading muskets.

Divided equally between the lines of Kafrdowar and Tel-el-Kebir were 80 Krupp guns and two field batteries, with *mitrailleuse* and rocket batteries at

Left: British soldiers cutting a dam constructed by Arabi at Mahuta.

both places; at Tel-el-Kebir were 12,000 infantry, chiefly young soldiers although said to be 'the flower of the army', plus 6,000 irregular Bedouins and a regiment of cavalry. Although Arabi had a basis of well-trained men and many field guns, rifles and stores, he lacked efficient officers and NCOs, but he did have unlimited numbers of excellent labourers to build military works. The emphasis on fortification at Kafrdowar, Tel-el-Kebir and other places undoubtedly arose from his sensible disinclination to meet the British in an open and general action; it was thought that if he held out until the Nile were high enough, he could cause infinite trouble. His artillery were Krupp field-pieces of the pattern used by the Prussians in their 1870 war against the French; they were only slightly inferior to the ordinary muzzle-loaders of the British artillery.

Graham's small force brushed aside resistance at Mahuta and entrenched at Kassassin, with Drury Lowe's Cavalry Brigade at Mehsameh, some miles to their rear. On 28 August, determined Egyptian attacks across the Canal were repulsed by the Royal Marine Artillery; the Egyptian infantry showed considerable skill in strengthening their left flank by moving along reverse slopes with only skirmishers on the skyline. Advancing in excellent attacking formation, they halted and dug a line of shelter-trenches about 1,000 yards from the British position, pushing infantry along the Canal to the left to within 900 yards of the York and Lancaster Regiment. Throughout their guns were extremely active and splendidly served, many shells bursting among the British troops. Fortunately, they were common shell with percussion fuzes which, when plumping deep into the soft sand, burst in such a fashion that few splinters flew upwards; later, when using shrapnel, the fuzes were badly cut causing the fire to be ineffective. Reinforced by 7th Dragoon Guards and three squadrons of Household Cavalry (Life Guards and Blues), in the evening Graham counter-attacked, and the heavy horsemen, cheering wildly, rode straight into the Egyptian infantry, trampling and sabring them into a disorganised retreat.

Arabi now withdrew behind the entrenched lines of Tel-el-Kebir, and in the next few weeks repeated skirmishes occurred between British and Indian cavalry against Regular Egyptian Horse, aided by Bedouins who fired from the saddle at long range;

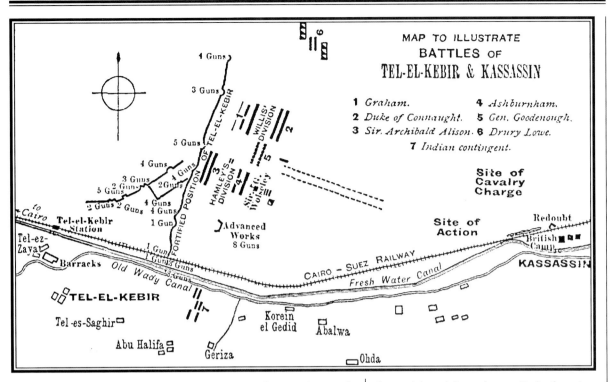

MAP TO ILLUSTRATE
BATTLES OF
TEL-EL-KEBIR & KASSASSIN

1 Graham.   4 Ashburnham.
2 Duke of Connaught.   5 Gen. Goodenough.
3 Sir. Archibald Alison. 6 Drury Lowe.
7 Indian contingent.

these brief encounters featured a creditable boldness and dash on the part of the Egyptian cavalry.

Constructed according to the most advanced principles of military engineering, on a 4-mile-long ridge, the lines of Tel-el-Kebir were garrisoned by about 22,000 men with numerous guns. Wolseley planned to tackle this formidable position at first light, after a 5½-mile night march at one mile per hour by his 17,000 men and 67 guns; beginning at 1.30 a.m. on 13 September. After hours of patient plodding through the soft, dragging sand, a paling of the sky showed dawn to be near. Dramatically the darkness was shattered by a torrent of firing from all along the Egyptian entrenchments; British bugles sounded the charge and relieved men filled the air with cheers as they dashed forward, bayonets fixed and without a shot being fired. Only 150 yards of open ground had to be covered, nevertheless nearly 200 men went down before reaching the 6-foot-wide, 4-foot-deep ditch fronting the 10-foot-high parapets. In the darkness, the Highland Brigade on the left of the attack went forward faster than the rest and were first to break into the enemy entrenchments; their bagpipes could be heard screeching above the tumult of battle as the Highlanders fought grimly with bayonet and rifle-butt. On the extreme right the Irish Regiments screamed wildly as they carried the position with the bayonet; while on the far side of the Canal the Indian Contingent met with little opposition and turned Arabi's right flank to complete the rout of his broken men. So quickly and successfully had the works been stormed that the Guards, in Wolseley's second line, did not fire a shot. Arabi lost his camp, stores and guns, suffered many casualties and his army was damaged beyond recovery.

The Egyptian infantry at Tel-el-Kebir were said to have borne the unexpected attack out of the darkness with the discipline and determination of first-class troops; the Highlanders, losing 243 out of the 339 casualties suffered by Wolseley's force, encountered strong resistance from the Egyptian Guard Regiment, which fell back silently and sullenly before them. Commanding the Highland Brigade, Sir Archibald Alison said: 'I must do justice to those much maligned Egyptian soldiers. I never saw men fight more steadily. They were falling back on an inner line of works which we had taken in flank and at every re-entering angle, at every battery and redoubt, they rallied and renewed, and I saw those poor men fighting hard when their officers were flying before us.' It was mostly the black Nubian infantry who fought well; hitherto stationed at Damietta whence they had come to reinforce Tel-el-Kebir, they were considered by many to be the best troops Arabi had, with a finer physique than the fellahin and better shots, their eyes being free from the chronic opthalmia of the Egyptians.

Tel-el-Kebir showed that while Egyptian soldiers were unable to meet Wolseley's men in open fighting, they were by no means to be despised when behind earthworks, and had Wolseley waited until daylight to deliver his attack, his losses would undoubtedly have been much heavier. Earlier, after the action at Kassassin, an attack from out of Tel-el-Kebir had impressed the correspondent of *The Standard* who wrote: 'It was impossible not to give the enemy credit for skilful tactics, and it was not from any fault of their leaders that the attack was unsuccessful. For a quarter of an hour, the position of our force and camp looked exceedingly critical, and our infantry were in eminent danger of being outflanked, until our cavalry forced the enemy back by moving round their flank.'

On the night of the day following the battle at Tel-el-Kebir, British cavalry made an arduous forced march of about forty miles, to enter Cairo just in time to save the city from destruction, and to capture Arabi himself. Their leader gone, and wearied with a war in which they had no substantial interest, the rebel army dispersed and the campaign was over.

Below: Lord Wolseley and his staff at the bridge of Tel-el-Kebir after the battle.

14
Chronology of the Rise of the Mahdi and the Sudan Expedition

1881: The appearance of the Mahdi

August: Mahdi's victory at Abba

October: Mahdi defeats Rashid Bey

1882, 29 May: Mahdists defeat Egyptians at Jebel Jarrada

1 September: Mahdists besiege El Obeid

1883, 1 January: Colonel W. Hicks appointed Egyptian Chief-of-Staff

17: El Obeid falls

29 April: Hicks' victorious action at Jebel Ain

9 September: Hicks marches out of Omdurman to recapture El Obeid

26 October: Mahdists destroy an Egyptian force

5 November: Hicks' army destroyed at Shaykan; Mahdists destroy another Egyptian force

2 December: Mahdists wipe out an Egyptian force; Slatin Pasha cut off in Darfur; Baker Pasha's force assembles at Suakim

1884, January: Lupton defeated at Bahrwel-Gazal; In Equatoria, Emin Pasha retreats up the Nile

10: Baring, in Cairo, rejects Gordon as Governor of Sudan

15: Wolseley interviews Gordon at the War Office

18: Gordon meets the Cabinet; later that day, leaves London for Cairo

25: In Cairo, Gordon meets Baring and Tewfik

26–7: Baker Pasha's force transported by sea to Trinkatat

28: Gordon leaves Cairo for Khartoum accompanied by Lieutenant-Colonel J. D. H. Stewart

1 February: They reach Korosko

4: Baker's force nearing Trinkatat

8: Admiral Hewitt lands a British force at Suakim with orders to mount expedition to relieve Tokar

10: Gordon sends Mahdi Red Robe of Honour

13: British troops in Egypt begin embarking for Suakim

18: Gordon and Stewart reach Khartoum

23: Tokar surrenders

28: Graham's force from Suakim concentrates at Trinkatat

29: Graham wins Battle of El Teb; Colonel Stewart and Mr. Power carry out, from Khartoum, a two-steamer reconnaissance on White Nile

2 March: Stewart and Power return to Khartoum

3: Graham's force reaches Tokar

5: Graham's force returns to Suakim

12: Graham's force marches out to Tamai

13: Graham victorious at Battle of Tamai; Telephone line from Khartoum to Cairo is cut by Mahdists; tribes north of Khartoum rise in support of Mahdi and Khartoum is cut off

14: Rebels take up positions on right bank of Blue Nile opposite palace at Khartoum

15: Besieged garrison of Hafiyeh (town north of Khartoum) relieved by Gordon's river force

16: Abortive sortie from Khartoum – 200 killed; British Government refuses Gordon's request that Zobeir be appointed Governor-General of Sudan

20: Khartoum besieged by 30,000 Arabs

22: Mahdi rejects Gordon's offer of peace

24: Baring, from Cairo, telegraphs London re importance of getting Gordon out of Khartoum

28: Graham's force at Suakim ordered to return to Egypt, leaving garrison of two battalions

3 **April:** Graham's force embarks for Egypt

9: They reach Cairo

9 **May:** Berber falls

10: Messengers confirm Khartoum tightly under siege and incommunicado

12: In London, Government survives vote of censure over its attitude and inactivity concerning Gordon and Khartoum

17: Message from Government reaches Gordon, advising evacuation of Khartoum

20: Public indignation in England at 'betrayal of Gordon'; continues throughout June and July

10 **June:** Confirmation of fall of Berber and massacre of its garrison

26 **July:** In England, Lord Hartington tells Gladstone he will resign unless help is sent to Gordon

5 **August:** Government votes funds for a Relief Expedition

8: Gladstone gives way, announces plans for an expedition to Sudan, commander Lord Wolseley; general movement of British regiments, *en route* to and from India, to Wadi Halfa; Muhammed Ali Pasha Husayn leads successful sorties from Khartoum

24: Letters from Gordon received, reporting minor actions with Arabs during period 12 March – 30 July; Gordon says he has received no messages since 29 March

26: Another letter from Gordon, announces a victory, by taking an Arab camp Khartoum is '… cleared on three parts of a circle'; on this day, General Redvers Buller leaves England for Egypt

28: Orders issued for construction of 800 whaling-gigs for the Nile Expedition

4 **September:** Expedition sent from Khartoum to Sennar is defeated with loss of 800 men at al Aylafuh

9: Wolseley arrives in Cairo

10: First whaling-gigs ready and delivered to U.K.; Steamer *Abbas* carrying Colonel Stewart and Frank Power leaves Khartoum; Expedition sent from Khartoum to recapture Berber is defeated with heavy losses

18: *Abbas* strikes rock. Stewart and Power go ashore and are murdered by apparently friendly Arabs

20: Gordon receives first news that relief expedition is on its way

27: Wolseley leaves Cairo for Wadi Halfa

7 **October:** Canadian *voyageurs* arrive at Alexandria

14: Gordon arrests sixteen leading citizens of Khartoum who have been planning to go over to the Mahdi

21: Mahdi moves to Khartoum with bulk of his forces

22: Gordon receives letter from Mahdi telling of wreck of *Abbas* and that Stewart and Power are dead

5 **December:** Relieving force assembles at Dongola

15: Steamer *Bordein*, under heavy fire, leaves Khartoum for Metemmeh; Gordon sends last message from Khartoum; General Stewart, with Mounted Infantry and Guards Camel Corps, arrives at Korti

16: Wolseley arrives at Korti

28: The River Column leaves Korti and begins advance towards Khartoum

30: Stewart's Desert Column leaves Korti to take the Wells at Gakdul

1885, 1 January: The first boats, bearing the Black Watch, reach Korti

2: Desert Column occupy the Wells at Gakdul

3: General Earle joins the advance-guard of his River Column

4: South Staffordshire Regiment passes Cataract and occupies Hamdab; joined by River Column, who camp there before moving forward; General Earle and Staff arrive at Hamdab

5: Lord Charles Beresford, RN, with 1st Division, Naval Brigade, reaches Korti; The Desert Column returns to Korti; at Khartoum, commander of the Omdurman Fort signals Gordon that he can hold out no longer; Gordon agrees to his surrendering

7: Colonel Clarke, with Light Camel Regiment, leaves Korti for Gakdul

8: Stewart's Desert Column marches out of Korti

13: United, the entire column moves forward

16: Discover large Arab force assembled at Abu Klea Wells

17: Stewart's force defeats Arabs at Abu Klea

18: The Column begins march to Metemmeh

19: Column come in sight of Nile at Abu Kru (Gubat) where Stewart is mortally wounded. Sir Charles Wilson takes command;

20: Force concentrates at Gubat

21: Wilson makes abortive attack on Metemmeh; Contact made with four river-steamers, sent down from Khartoum by Gordon

24: River Column leaves Hamdab; Wilson takes a party from the Desert Column up the Nile in two steamers *Bordein* and *Talahawiyeh*

25–26: Mahdi's forces attack Khar-toum; the city falls and Gordon killed; Wilson's force in *Bordein* aground *en route* to Khartoum.

26: *Bordein* refloated

27: Buller, with Royal Irish Regiment, begins desert march to Gubat

28: Wilson's steamers arrive at junction of Blue and White Niles; *Bordein* leads way into Khartoum, heavily engaged from shore; finding Khartoum in enemy hands, Wilson orders retreat

29: *Talahawiyeh* hits rocks and sinks

31: At Cataract near Wad Habashi, *Bordein* hits rocks and is abandoned; troops make camp on nearby island and small boat rows forty miles to Gubat for assistance

1 February: Boat reaches Gubat; Lord Charles Beresford sets out in steamer *Safieh* to find Wilson

3: *Safieh* damaged by fire from shore; after repairs, carries on to reach Wilson

4: Beresford finds Wilson and returns to Korti with him and his party; Desert Column concentrates at Birti

5: Force ordered to halt on hearing of fall of Khartoum; Government in London hear of fall of city and Gordon's death

6: *Safieh* reaches Desert Column's camp

8: Earle receives message from Wolseley ordering him to push on to Abu Hamed; Earle decides to abandon boats and march across desert

9: On being told that force is to be detailed for an advance to Suakim, Wolseley asks for an Indian Brigade and cavalry

11: Buller and the Royal Irish Regiment arrive at Gubat from Korti; the Nile Column wins Battle of Kirbekan; Earle is killed, General Brackenbury takes command

17: General Stewart dies of wounds received on 19 January; River Column march resumed and reaches Es Salamat

19: Queen Victoria inspects Grenadier Guards at Windsor, before they leave for Sudan

20: Brackenbury's force reaches El Hebba

23: Buller evacuates Abu Klea

24: Brackenbury within 26 miles of Abu Hamed

26: Buller's column reaches Gakdul

4 March: Brackenbury's forces arrive at Hamdab

5: They reach Merowe

6: Brackenbury holds final review of River Column

7: He leaves with main body for Korti

8: The Desert Column sets out for Korti

12: General Graham arrives in Suakim

16: Commencement of laying of Suakim–Berber railway line; Desert Column reaches Korti

20: Graham's force begin advance from Suakim to Hasin

21: Graham victorious at Battle of Hasin

22: Graham's force surprised at Tofrik; win hard-fought battle; Troops leave Korti for Cairo

29: Australian Contingent arrives at Suakim

1 April: Graham's force advances to Tamai; finds no enemy

4: Force returns to Suakim

2 May: Wolseley arrives at Suakim

17: General Graham and Staff embark from Suakim

19: Wolseley and Staff embark from Suakim; Australians embark for home

2 June: Australian force arrives Sydney

8: Wolseley and General Graham back in Britain

29: Death of the Mahdi

6 July: British forces re-assemble in Egypt

Left: The Mahdi

15
The Expedition to the Sudan, 1883–5

Right: Osman Digna.

After Wolseley's successful campaign, the British virtual occupation of Egypt involved them in the Sudan where control had been slipping from the Egyptian Government's hands to those of the Muslim prophet, the Mahdi. Following the British Government's refusal to intervene in the Sudan in 1882, the Egyptian Government engaged Colonel W. Hicks, a retired officer of the Indian Army, who marched into the Kordofan desert in September 1883 at the head of some 10,000 disorganised Egyptian troops re-enlisted from the defeated army of Arabi. In November near El Obeid this force was utterly destroyed by a greatly superior force of Sudanese tribesmen, which left Khartoum and all the country to its south at the Mahdi's mercy.

Leading a large force of tribesmen, Osman Digna besieged Sinkat, about 60 miles from Suakim, cutting to pieces an Egyptian relief force on 6 November and another near Tamai on 2 December. The Egyptian Government now appointed Major-General Valentine Baker, head of the Egyptian police, to march to Suakim with a force of 4,000 men – in fact, a rabble of policemen and peasants. Near El Teb the force was attacked by Osman Digna and about 1,200 Sudanese tribesmen who displayed the most reckless bravery while the Egyptians showed the most craven cowardice. In almost indescribable confusion, with cavalry, infantry, mules, camels, baggage and casualties crushed into a struggling and surging mass, the Egyptian soldiers allowed themselves to be slaughtered by natives inferior to them in numbers and armed only with spears and swords. Unable to rally the Egyptian soldiers and realising that the position was hopeless, Baker and some of his staff hewed their way out of the struggling mass leaving behind 112 officers and 2,250 men killed and wounded besides losing their machine-guns, field-guns and 3,000 rifles. Four days later the besieged force at Sinkat were

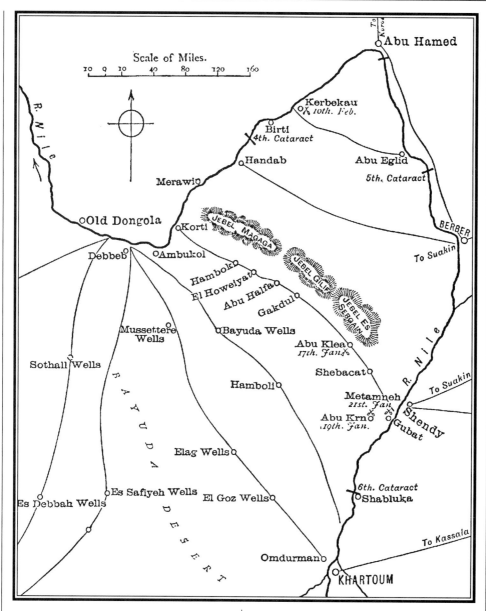

destroyed as they attempted to fight their way out.

Deeming themselves in honour bound to save the garrison of Khartoum, while evacuating the Sudan, the British Government sent General Charles Gordon, a former Governor-General of the Sudan, to Khartoum. At the same time Major-General Sir Gerald Graham, V.C. was given command of an expedition against Osman Digna, consisting of two brigades of British infantry (under Major-General Sir Redvers Buller, V.C. and Major-General Davis), some cavalry including the 10th Hussars, eight 7-pounder guns and six Gatling guns – a total of about 4,000 men.

On 29 February 1884 the force marched out from Trinkitat in a square formation with guns and Gatlings at the corners, cavalry and

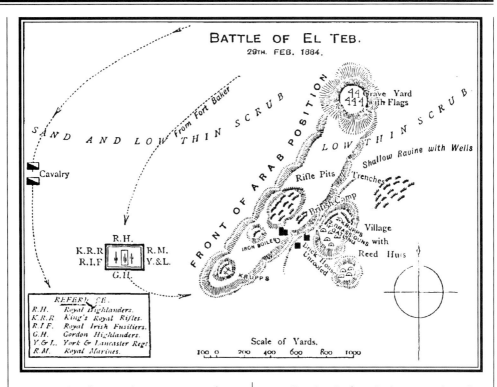

mounted infantry thrown out to front and flanks and guarding the rear. The transport animals, carrying ammunition and medical supplies, were in the centre of the formation. The huge square plodded over the barren sandy soil to come upon the enemy positioned near El Teb, not far from the decomposing heaps of mutilated bodies of Baker's annihilated army. The Sudanese tribesmen were positioned in shallow earthworks and rifle pits and a fortified building in front of the village and wells of El Teb. The bugles sounded the advance and the bagpipes struck up as Graham marched his square to the right in an attempt to turn the enemy's left. The guns captured from Baker Pasha poured out a storm of shrapnel shells – they were served by impressed artillerymen from the garrison of Tokar, recently taken by the Dervishes. The formation slowly plodded forward for about 1,000 yards with shells bursting over it and bullets bringing down men on all sides before halting so that the men could lie down while casualties were treated.

It was noon and very hot as Graham brought his guns into action at 900 yards' range and, together with the rattling Gatlings, they soon silenced the two Krupp guns. Then the square got to its feet and moved forward without losing cohesion in a shoulder-to-shoulder wheeling movement towards the enemy left flank that brought the Black Watch to the front from their original position at the rear face. As the British infantry neared the defences, vast numbers of tribesmen threw aside their rifles and flourishing broad-bladed spears and cross-hilted swords, flung themselves like a swarm of furious bees upon the levelled bayonets of the square, only to be cut down in dozens by the fire of the Martini rifles and the Gatlings. To stop the fierce onrushing natives some of the British soldiers had sliced off the heads of their bullets, but even the huge wounds caused by these expanding 'dum-dum' missiles failed to halt the courageous tribesmen.

Colonel Fred Burnaby of the Blues (out in the desert on 'sick-leave') picked them off like driven hares with a double-barrelled twelve-bore loaded with pig-shot which brought down thirteen natives for an expenditure of 23 cartridges. The few Sudanese who reached the square engaged in a sharp hand-to-hand fight until they were repelled and swept by fire as they ran back. The square continued to move forward and carried the entrenchments, turning the captured guns of one Arab battery on to those of the second, then halted, reformed itself and advanced slowly but steadily on the second drab line of trenches and rifle pits. As they had done before, the Sudanese came out of their holes and flung themselves upon the British who were in two long lines as Graham deployed his flanks. The fortified building was carried by a brilliant charge of the Naval Landing Party as every inch of ground was contested by the Sudanese who seemed to spring out of the ground like rabbits.

While the infantry fight had been going on, Stewart's cavalry had swept round the enemy's right flank, dashing after them in three lines while the tribesmen split into two large bodies to right and left so that the Hussars had a gallop of three miles before catching them. The tribesmen flung themselves on the ground as the cavalry passed, attempting to hamstring the horses and throwing boomerangs of mimosa wood at their legs. On one occasion, thirty Arab horsemen, riding bare-backed and armed with two-edged swords, charged a whole squadron but were wiped out after causing casualties. The Hussars found it almost impossible to reach the crouching or lying Arabs with their sabres and later General Stewart adapted Arab spears

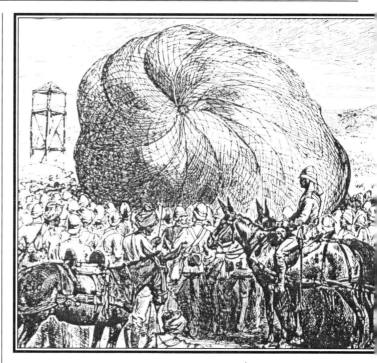

Above: The march to Tamai – inflating the recconnaissance balloon.

as lances by weighting the heads with a roll of iron.

By 2 p.m. the position was taken and the Sudanese were streaming away towards Tokar, having lost more than 2,000 men in a convincing demonstration of the superiority of discipline backed by Martini rifles and machine-guns over numerical strength and fanatical courage. The British had 34 killed and 155 wounded.

Finding Osman Digna's force in position near the village and wells of Tamai, Graham marched out on 15 March with his whole force in two squares in echelon from the left, with Davis's 2nd Brigade leading and Buller's 1st Brigade on its right rear so that the two squadrons could support each other with fire. After marching for some time over a rough plain, Davis's square was suddenly assailed by large parties of tribesmen in fierce rushes. The men frantically opened fire and, despite bugle calls and orders from the officers, could not be persuaded to reserve their fire or to aim steadily. In

a few minutes dense clouds of smoke hung on the still air, hiding the enemy and allowed them to creep up unseen. Those companies of the York and Lancasters and the Black Watch forming the front face of Davis's square had moved forward more quickly than their remaining companies who formed the sides of the square so that gaps appeared in what should have been a solid wall of men. Under the cover of the smoke, large groups of the enemy burst from the haze of dust and smoke to rush upon the right-angle of the square, creeping and crawling beneath the bayonets and muzzles of the Gatling guns to enter the square and push it back in wild confusion. Broken up into small groups of men fighting for their lives while officers strove to reorganise their men, the confused mass recoiled as the sheer weight of the attack forced them back. The machine-guns of the Naval Brigade were captured but not before they had been locked by their crew who stood by them till the last. Left without protection, the gunners of the battery of four guns stood firm and mowed down the onrushing tribesmen with shrapnel. Highlanders, formed into small groups that disputed every inch of the ground, gradually checked the retreat until the men began to rally and reform to the shouted orders of officers and sergeants.

Five hundred yards to the right rear, Buller's square was being attacked in the same furious manner, but by sheer fire power literally blew away the enemy as they approached. Then the Gordons, Royal Irish and Rifles poured a steady fire across the open ground at the tribesmen attacking Davis's square. Stewart galloped his cavalry round to the left flank of the square and dismounted his men who, opening fire with their carbines, caught the tribesmen between two fires. At last they wavered and stopped coming forward and, after fresh ammunition had been brought out, the 2nd Brigade formed in line and moved forward again to the attack to recapture the guns and turn them on the enemy. Large numbers of tribesmen attacked furiously from a broad and deep ravine where they had been lying concealed, but melted away as the troops, again in squares, poured in crashing volleys. Finally, they were routed by the cavalry who swept round their left flank and dismounted to pour volley after volley into their backs.

Amid wounded natives lying thickly among the scrub, firing or slashing at anyone who came within reach, Graham's force reformed and began to advance on Tamai, about three miles

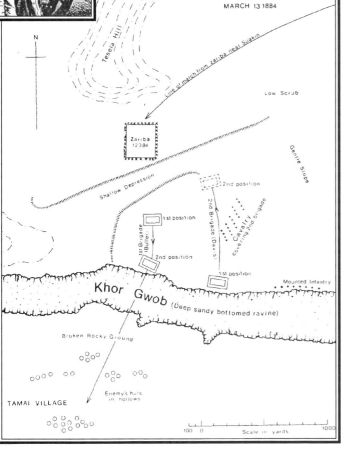

BATTLE OF TAMAI
MARCH 13 1884

from the battlefield. On occasions groups of the enemy seemed about to attack but were turned back by artillery fire. Buller's brigade destroyed Osman's camp while Davis's battered brigade returned to the *zareba* occupied on the previous night. During the fighting the British had lost 109 killed and 102 wounded in beating off an estimated force of about 9,000 natives of whom 2,000 were killed.

The victory at Tamai opened the road from Suakim to Berber on the Nile, which was still held by an Egyptian garrison. There was perhaps a fleeting opportunity to reach Khartoum, but Graham's telegraphic request was turned down by the Government. On 28 March, after several skirmishes with the enemy, he received instructions that the campaign was to be brought to a close. So, leaving two British battalions to garrison Suakim, on 3 April Graham embarked the remainder of his force and sailed for Egypt.

Following Graham's withdrawal from Suakim, the British Government belatedly decided to send an expedition under General Sir Garnet Wolseley to relieve Khartoum. He reached Cairo on 9 September 1884. Recalling his Red River Campaign, Wolseley decided that the force of 7,000 men should go up the Nile in small boats manned by *voyageurs*, boatmen hired from Canada. Eight hundred boats each 30 feet long and 6 feet 6 inches in the beam were ordered from 47 British shipyards and these arrived in Alexandria in nineteen sepa-

rate ships. Contracted to transport the entire army as far as the Second Cataract, the paddle-steamers of Messrs Thomas Cook towed lines of boats, like beads on a string, upstream to Wadi Halfa. Crewed by two *voyageurs*, each boat carried ten soldiers, sitting comfortably under awnings smoking their pipes and trailing their hands in the water, together with their equipment. But from the Second Cataract onwards, the soldiers had to laboriously pull at the oars for many hours, hardly moving the boats against the strong current. The Royal Irish Regiment won the prize of one hundred pounds offered by Wolseley to the battalion that would make the quickest passage in its boat up to Korti. Thousands of natives struggled along the steep and rocky banks, encouraged by Egyptian soldiers with whips, as the paddle-steamers, steel hawsers slung under their hulls, were manhandled past the Second Cataract. By the middle of December the bulk of the expeditionary force was gathered at Korti where a large camp was formed.

Wolseley divided his force into two columns: the River Column under Major-General Earle, consisting of 2,200 men with six screw-guns, to proceed up the Nile by boat and then open up the desert road between Abu Hamed and Korosko, finally pushing on to Berber to co-operate with the second column. The latter was commanded by Brigadier-General Sir Herbert Stewart and had the task of

Right: An Egyptian gunboat on the Nile, 1884.

Left: General Sir Garnet Wolseley.

making their way straight across the Bayuda desert to Metemmeh to open up another and more direct road to Khartoum. Totalling 2,000 men with about 300 camel drivers and native porters, it included a Naval Brigade and a squadron of the 19th Hussars mounted on horses, together with the Royal Sussex Regiment, a company of the Essex Regiment, some Royal Engineers and half a battery of Royal Artillery. A unique element of the force was its Camel Corps. Proposed by Wolseley and accepted by the War Office, it consisted of specially picked men from the Grenadier, Coldstream and Scots Guards and the Royal Marines, who together formed: the Guards Camel Regiment; the Heavy Camel Regiment of selected men from the Household Cavalry Regiments and other crack cavalry units; and the Mounted Infantry Camel Regiment composed of specially chosen men from various infantry regiments, most of whom had previously served in South Africa or Egypt. Before the col-

umn could leave, the Camel Corps had to be trained to ride their camels. About thirty red tunics were taken to be worn by those who were to proceed on the first steamer from Metemmeh to Khartoum with the idea of impressing and perhaps terrifying the Mahdi and his followers.

On 30 December Stewart moved out to occupy the Wells of Gakdul. The great phalanx of camels, forty abreast, ambled forward in a solid column that extended for half a mile, the centre composed of 800 baggage camels driven by natives from Aden dressed in red turbans, blue jerseys and big brass identification labels. Three 7-pounder guns were with the column and 30 of Beresford's Blue Jackets were dragging a Gardner gun.

After a difficult journey with considerable loss of camels, the Desert Column reached Gakdul on 12 January and, leaving a detachment of the Sussex Regiment to hold the wells, moved forward to the Abu Klea valley. On the morning of 17 January

1885, Stewart formed his force of 1,500 officers and men with three screw-guns and one Gardner gun into a huge square with the camels in the middle, and slowly marched off down the valley towards a row of coloured banners which stretched across it. It was a very hot day and the going was rough. Frequently the square had to halt to enable the doctors to attend to casualties from the harassing fire of the enemy, and to redress the form of the square so as to prevent its rear face being forced out by the sluggish camels. Then the banners stirred as their bearers stood up and the Dervish army of 15,000 warriors lay before them in battle array. Suddenly and dramatically, the air was filled with shouting, screaming and the beating of drums.

Five hundred yards from the flags the square halted to dress its rear face. The shouting died away and a large section of the enemy army rushed forward in a serrated line, charging down in silence towards the left front corner of the square, the furious drumming of their bare feet making the ground quiver. Although wave after wave of them went down before the fire of the Martinis and the Gardner guns, still they came on. As they neared the square, the Dervishes changed direction and came swiftly down on its most vulnerable point, the left rear corner where it had been bulged out by the camels and 'gapped' by the Gardner gun which had been run out about 20 yards by the Naval Brigade. Even the massed volleys of rifle fire could not did halt the assailants and in a few seconds this corner of the square was pressed back by sheer weight of numbers. The Gardner guns jammed and at least half the Naval Brigade were slaughtered as they fought around it. Colonel Burnaby was killed while fighting outside the square and General Stewart was only rescued with consid-

erable difficulty when his horse was shot from under him. Many of the infantry rifles jammed through heat and rapid firing leaving the men with only a bayonet, which frequently bent, to fight off the fanatical tribesmen.

Disordered and thrown into momentary confusion, the square was only saved by the stability of the Guards who held their ground on the two sides that were not being attacked. Setting their feet apart and putting their rear rank about, the Guardsmen shot down or bayoneted every native who approached them. As the left face of the square was gradually forced back to the rear of the front face, and the rear face was forced in, the camels formed a living traverse that broke the Arab rush and gave the defenders time to reform. The centre of the square was a scene of desperate conflict with camels, horses and men forming a slashing, hacking, surging mass. Lord Charles Beresford, trying to clear the jammed Gardner

Above: The death of Burnaby at Abu Klea, 17 January 1885.

gun, was knocked down and carried against the face of the square by sheer weight of numbers. One rank of the formation was forced up a steep little mound which enabled the rear rank to open fire over the heads of the front rank men and relieve the pressure. Finally the enemy momentarily wavered and then, in dignified fashion, slowly walked away from the square, turning their backs upon it and leaving great piles of their dead behind them. After a battle that had lasted only five minutes, no fewer than 1,100 dead tribesmen were counted in the immediate neighbourhood of the square, while the British had lost 74 officers and men killed and about 100 wounded. Several Victoria Crosses were awarded for this action.

The muddy water at the Wells of Abu-Klea tasted like champagne, but the column spent a cold and miserable night as no stores or baggage had come up. Next morning, leaving the wounded behind in a small improvised fort guarded by 100 men of the Royal Sussex Regiment, the column marched off to Metemmeh about 23 miles away. It was a very distressing march over rough ground and not until 7.30 a.m. on the following day was a gravel ridge topped to reveal the Nile stretching ribbon-like before them, with a large force of tribesmen positioned between the column and the river. General Stewart said: 'First we will have breakfast and then go out to fight,' and the troops sat down on the sand to eat their breakfast under a falling shower of long-range bullets. It was now that Stewart was struck in the groin and mortally wounded; command of the column was taken over by Sir Charles Wilson.

Leaving the 'Heavies' – the 19th Hussars – the Royal Artillery and the Naval Brigade with their guns and the Gardner gun in a fortified redoubt made of boxes and rocks on a hillock, the rest of the column formed up in square and marched out at two o'clock in the afternoon. Reinforced from Omdurman, the tribesmen were in great strength and their banners rose out of the long grass on all sides. Whenever they revealed themselves the guns in the *zareba* opened up on them while the Gardner gun kept grinding away. As suddenly as at Abu

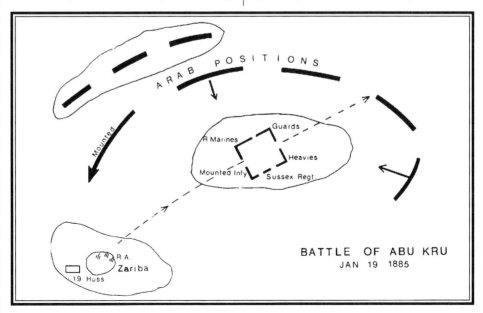

BATTLE OF ABU KRU
JAN 19 1885

Klea, the enemy came pounding down the hill with several horsemen in the lead. The square halted to receive the charge and, spontaneously cheering, the men began frantically firing. Then bugles sounded the cease-fire and, surprisingly, the men obeyed the call. Steadied by the momentary rest, they resumed firing with deadly effect so that not a single tribesman got within 50 yards of the square. In a few minutes the entire front ranks of the enemy were swept away and, hastily turning, the Dervishes disappeared. The British force had lost one officer and 22 men killed and eight officers and 90 men wounded. Reaching the river, the men fell like logs and buried their faces in the muddy water.

The troops bivouacked on the river bank that night and early next morning formed up and marched back to the zareba where there had been considerable fighting on the previous day. Reunited, the whole force marched away in columns of regiments carrying 25 wounded men on hand-stretchers because of shortage of camels. Although hovering around the flanks, the enemy did not attack again in force and the column reached the river village of Abu-Kru by nightfall where the wounded were placed in huts and the houses were loopholed for defence. At dawn on 21 January, Sir Charles Wilson advanced with 1,000 men in double column to take the well-defended town of Metemmeh, but retired after some fighting, leaving the town in enemy hands.

The force was now joined by four armoured river-steamers sent down by Gordon from Khartoum, and the next two days were spent overhauling them, collecting wood for fuel and reconnoitring. On the morning of 24 January 1885, the Bordein and the Talahawiyeh churned up the Nile towards Khartoum. The two steamers carried twenty men of the Royal Sussex, some naval personnel and about 200 Sudanese infantry; the Talahawiyeh towed a barge loaded with grain. Sir Charles Wilson was in Bordein. For three days the heavily laden vessels slowly made their way up river, moving only by day, frequently running aground and fighting skirmishes with enemy on the banks and often stopping to pull down wooden houses to use as fuel. At first light on 27 January, the towers of Khartoum could be seen in the far distance and a heavy fire was opened on the steamers from four guns and thousands of rifles at a range of about 600 yards. With boilers straining almost to the bursting point, running the gauntlet of guns and rifle fire from batteries on both banks, the vessels, bearing their now red-coated British infantry, pressed upstream to swing laboriously in sight of Khartoum. The lack of welcome was ample evidence that the town had fallen – it had been stormed two days earlier and Gordon had been killed.

Wilson ordered the steamers to turn and run full steam down river, running a gauntlet of fire from both banks until four o'clock in the afternoon. With heavy hearts, the crews worked the steamers through the cataracts, sunken rocks and sand banks, losing Talahawiyeh when she hit a submerged rock. On 31 January the last rapid was overcome, leaving a clear stretch of smooth water all the way to Metemmeh. In the afternoon the Bordein hit a submerged rock and had to be laid alongside a sandspit running out from an island where guns, ammunition and stores were quickly landed. Wilson entrenched his small force on the island and sent a ship's boat downstream to get help from the Desert Column, which was reached in the early morning of 1 February.

That afternoon Lord Charles Beresford took the small river steamer Safieh up the Nile with a crew that included twenty picked marksmen of the Rifles, two Gardner guns and two 4-pounders. On the third morning *Safieh* ran the gauntlet of Arab earthworks at Wadi Habeshi, passing within 30 yards of the entrenchments and pouring such showers of shells and bullets into them that the Arabs were unable to reply until the little steamer was 200 yards past them when a well-directed shot from an Arab gun went through the stern and into one of the boilers. Beresford managed to get *Safieh* further up-stream and anchored stern-on to the enemy at about 500 yards' range. Throughout the day a firefight was carried on between the steamer and the Arabs on shore. At daybreak next morning, with the boiler repaired, Beresford was able to embark Sir Charles Wilson and his party who had come down the right bank. Without further loss, *Safieh* reached the Desert Column's camp on the evening of 6 February.

To build the railway from Suakim on the sea to Berber on the Nile, it was essential to crush Osman Digna's forces of 7,000 men at Tamai, 3,000 men at Hasin (six miles west of Suakim) and a small garrison at Tokar. Lieutenant-General Sir Gerald Graham arrived at Suakim on 12 March 1885 to command a force of about 13,000 fighting men, consisting of 1st Guards Infantry Brigade and a Line Brigade formed of the East Surreys, the Shropshires, the Berkshires and the Royal Marines. There was a cavalry brigade of four squadrons of the 5th Lancers and the 25th Hussars; some Mounted Infantry; Engineer detachments and an Indian contingent formed of the 15th Sikhs, 9th Bengal Cavalry, 17th and 28th Native Infantry and a company of Madras Sappers. Later a force of 500 infantry and artillery arrived from New South Wales in Australia. There were also 11,000 camp-followers.

The port of Suakim was crowded with naval vessels, troopships, transports and hospital ships, and special vessels for condensing 85,000 gallons of water a day for the troops. Some 6,000 baggage and 500 riding camels with their headmen and drivers were gathered from India, Egypt and Aden, and mules were brought from Gibraltar, Malta and Cyprus. The fighting men were almost lost in the multitudes of camp-followers and labourers working on the railway.

Leaving the Shropshires to garrison Suakim, Graham marched out on 20 March with his force formed as three sides of a square made up of more than 8,000 officers and men with 1,192 horses, 210 mules, 735 camels and ten guns, with cavalry covering the front and flanks. Graham's objective was the Wells at Hasin whence a force could threaten the right flank of any British column moving southwestwards. Over rough ground scattered with small boulders and prickly mimosa bushes, the force made a most exhausting march on a very hot day until they debouched from a pass on to a spacious plan encircled by craggy hills. Banners waving and weapons flashing in the sunlight, the Arabs could be seen posted in great strength on a spur to their left front. The bushes were alive with riflemen who swarmed through the undergrowth, showing very little of themselves except puffs of smoke rising above the mimosa bushes. The Berkshires and the Marines dashed forward in gallant style to assault the enemy's position on some hillocks to the right of the ridge occupied by the tribesmen. The Marines reached the crest first and covered the advance of the Berkshires by rolling volleys of musketry which re-echoed among the surrounding hills.

Forced from their position, the Arabs retired across the plain towards Tamai, harassed by two squadrons of Bengal Lancers while two more squadrons of Bengal Cavalry and the 5th Lancers completely scattered a group of the enemy on the right who were trying to turn the British flank via the Hasin Valley. Through weight of numbers, the Bengal Lancers on the left were forced to retire on to the Guards' square which had been posted as a reserve in the rear. Racing after the retiring horsemen, the Arabs suddenly came upon this square and attacked it without a moment's hesitation, but not one of the 3,000 Arab spearmen and riflemen got nearer than 15 or 20 yards, beaten back by crashing volleys of musketry.

Leaving the East Surreys to hold the hill-tops commanding the Hasin wells, Graham's infantry brigades returned in square covered by the Horse Artillery while parties of Arabs galled them with fire from the bushes. British losses were one officer and eight men killed, three officers and 36 men wounded; the Arabs lost an estimated 1,000 men.

Next Graham sent out a force to build and garrison two *zareba*s as intermediate supply posts in the desert. Under Major-General Sir John McNeill, V.C., it consisted of a squadron of the 5th Lancers, the Berkshire Regiment, Royal Marines; a detachment of the Naval Brigade with four Gardner guns, and an Indian Brigade of Infantry with a large convoy of camels, and an engineer detachment who laid a telegraph line as the troops advanced. Formed in two squares, the force advanced slowly through dense scrub and mimosa bush and by noon had only reached Tofrik, six miles from Suakim. McNeill realised that he could not build the *zareba* at the arranged eight miles point before dusk, so he telegraphed Graham for permission to make a *zareba* at Tofrik. He planned to form three separate squares of mimosa-thorn fence placed diagonally like a chess board with the large central square housing the transport animals and stores while the two smaller flanking squares held the fighting troops and Gardner guns. Under the protection of a screen of infantry pickets and cavalry, who reported that the enemy to their front were in small parties and retiring towards Tamai, the flanking squares were built and surrounding bush was cleared amid oppressive heat. The Marines were working on the northern flanking square with two Gardner guns; the Berkshires were in the southern flanking square with the other two Gardners, both with their arms piled. At 2 o'clock, when the men fell out by half-battalions to eat their dinner, there was no proper field of fire around the incomplete defences. The Indian Infantry were in the area of the unfinished central square where the camels and mules were assembled after off-loading.

At 2.30 p.m. cavalrymen came galloping in to report that the enemy were advancing rapidly; at their heels came the cavalry outposts fleeing through the working parties under heavy fire from natives who seemed to have sprung, screaming and shouting, from the very earth. Thousands of Arabs had crept up unnoticed through the rocks and scrub while the shirt-sleeved infantrymen were working on the *zareba,* their arms piled some yards away. With a hoarse roar, 5,000 glistening black Hadendowahs rose to their feet and flooded in, hacking and stabbing as they hit the bunched camels, causing them to shy away and then crowd down upon the startled infantrymen like floodwater from a burst dam, throwing into disorder the Native Infantry who fired a volley and then broke and rushed towards the central square. Then the plain became covered with riderless horses, camels and mules tearing towards Suakim, as the working parties rushed to their weapons. The main attack was directed at the *zarebas* of the Berk-

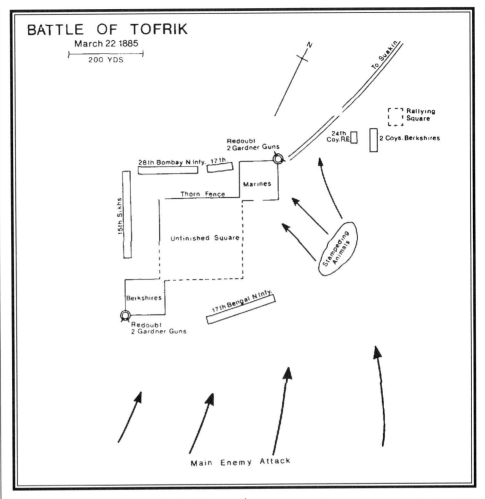

BATTLE OF TOFRIK
March 22 1885
200 YDS

To Suakin

N

Rallying Square

24th Coy.RE

2 Coys.Berkshires

Redoubt 2 Gardner Guns

28th Bombay N Infy. 17th.

15th Sikhs

Marines

Thorn Fence

Unfinished Square

Berkshires

Stampeding Animals

Redoubt 2 Gardner Guns

17th Bengal N Infy.

Main Enemy Attack

shires where General McNeill was lucky to escape with his life. A group of Berkshires outside the central *zareba* formed square and, holding their fire until the Arabs were within 30 yards, mowed down the tribesmen milling around the small formation that slowly fell back upon the Marines' *zareba*, frequently halting to fire volleys into the enemy at close range.

In the first rush, some 60 Arabs penetrated the Marines' square and were instantly shot or bayoneted, but an avalanche of Arabs, fleeing Indian Infantry, camp-followers and animals burst through the central square sweeping away many of the formed soldiers. Because the tribesmen were amongst the transport animals, the Berkshires and Marines were forced to fire heavy volleys into them. Camels reared their great bodies into the air before slumping into shapeless tawny masses on the blood-soaked sand. The space marked out for the central *zareba* was a hideous chaos of shouting, demoralised men, frantic camels and plunging kicking mules while the shapeless forms of Hadendowah warriors flitted amid clouds of dust, cleaving paths through the mass with their long, razor-sharp swords.

Remaining firm, the 15th Sikhs and 28th Bombay Native Infantry maintained an intact line to receive and repel successive assaults. Thrown back, large bodies of the enemy milled around in all directions, charging at the *zareba* fence, slashing at the helpless camp-followers, gashing and hamstringing camels and mules until at last, turned back by the concentrated fire from the Marines and Berkshires' squares, the surviving Hadendowahs slowly and sullenly retreated from the area of fighting and walked away into the bush.

The twenty minutes that the battle had lasted was crowded with instances of cool bravery, wild bewilderment and fanatical desperation. As the smoke and dust cleared away a shambles of dead men and animals was revealed. The British lost 100 men killed and 140 wounded, and 900 camels destroyed, while at least 1,000 of the enemy lay dead around and within the *zareba*s.

The night was very dark and the tense troops were prevented from sleeping by the moans and cries of the wounded, and the bullets that came whizzing into the camp, fired by tribesmen who still infested the bush around them. Next morning, General Graham came up with the Brigade of Guards and for the next eight days the men were kept busy clearing the battlefield and rebuilding the *zareba* to take a garrison of one battalion. Water was scarce and men collapsed in dozens from sunstroke. The tribesmen's confidence had been shaken by their reverse and the campaign was tailing off into a series of marches and counter-marches, convoy-escorting, *zareba*-building and skirmishes – the New South Wales contingent comporting themselves with gallantry in one such affair at Dhakdul.

Observation was kept by a captive balloon filled from gas cylinders and towed by a rope attached to a wagon drawn by horses in the centre of the moving square of men. At a height of 300–400 feet, it was possible to have a perfect observation of the surrounding country and notes were sent down tied to a long cord.

On 3 April Graham advanced unhindered towards Osman Digna's headquarters at Tamai, finding the villages deserted and the wells almost dry. Most of the tribes had deserted Digna, who was on his way to Sinkat, and defensive operations were now practically at an end.

On 2 January 1885 Earle's River Column had moved away from Korti. It consisted of a squadron of 19th Hussars, the Staffordshire Regiment, Black Watch, Gordon Highlanders, Duke of Cornwall's Light Infantry, a battery of Egyptian artillery and the Egyptian Camel Corps. With the Hussars on the left and the Camel Corps on the right bank, the heavy whalers battled against rocks and cataracts – it took the burly soldiers of the Black Watch four days to work their way through a cataract seven miles in length. Frequently the boats had to be portaged – everything removed from them, they were carried along the rough rock-strewn banks for a mile or more; at times the crews of three boats hauled a single whaler through the rocks of the swift flowing river.

Leaving the boats and marching through the desert towards Abu-Hamed, Earle found his path blocked by the enemy strongly positioned on the Kirbekan ridge. he decided to make a feigned frontal attack while sending six companies each of the Staffords and Black Watch with the Hussars round the left flank to take the enemy in rear. Earle himself accompanied the flanking column which, although seen and under fire for much of their route, managed to get into position so as effectively to turn the enemy position by taking it in rear and overlapping it on the right flank. The guns of the false frontal attack could be heard as the Staffords and Highlanders, with pipes skirling, stormed the heights at the point of the bayonet. While searching the crest for Arabs hiding in holes or behind rocks, they came upon a stone hut, from which a tribesmen shot and killed General Earle.

While the fighting on the heights was going on, the Hussars rode off and captured the enemy camp at the entrance to the nearby Shukook Pass. The entire operation cost 3 officers and 9 men killed, 4 officers and 44 men wounded against an estimated Arab loss of hundreds.

For twelve more days the force struggled up river towards Abu-Hamed, which they would probably have captured together with Berber, but on 24 February they were ordered by Wolseley to return. On 8 March the force arrived back at Korti, after taking only nine days for the downstream voyage (although several lives were lost) against 31 days to ascend the cataracts. During this period Redvers Buller's Desert Column had been effecting a masterly retirement from its position on the Nile near Metemmeh, the marching square repeatedly fending off small-scale Arab attacks.

On 2 May, Wolseley arrived in Suakim to announce that the Government had suspended the building of the railway and that they were to retire from the Sudan altogether, leaving only a garrison at Suakim. By midday, Korti was completely evacuated, its forts and large buildings being destroyed as the troops retired. Buller superintended the arrangements until 17 June when he handed over command of the rearguard to General Brackenbury. In June the Mahdi died of typhus; Wolseley returned to England and the Nile Expedition was at an end.

Having succeeded Sir Evelyn Wood as Sirdar of the Egyptian Army, Major-General Sir Francis Grenfell was busily forming a Nile Frontier Force of British and Egyptian troops. Towards the end of November 1885, the Khalifa Abdul-lahi, the Mahdi's successor, appeared with a Dervish army a few miles south of Ginnis and British posts at Kosha and Mograka were attacked. General Sir Frederick Stephenson, with two British brigades, attacked and defeated the enemy at Ginnis on the penultimate day of 1885 – it was the very last occasion on which British troops went into action wearing scarlet tunics. Not a very great battle, it was the first time that Egyptian troops had fought the Dervishes to a standstill although they were backed by some English regiments, including the Cameron Highlanders. The surprised Mahdi retired with his army behind the Third Cataract.

Three years of raid and counter-raid ensued, with Egyptian troops gaining strength and confidence as the British regiments were withdrawn. On 28 April 1887, Lieutenant-Colonel Chermside led an all-Egyptian force on a night march to wipe out a strong Dervish army at Saras and greatly raised the morale of the Egyptian army as it was the very first occasion on which Egyptian Regular troops, without British support, had fought the Dervishes. In mid-1889, the Mahdi attempted to invade Egypt and isolate Wadi Halfa by sending a force through the Western Desert to the Nile, 25 miles north of Aswan. At Toski on 3 August 1889, the Dervishes under the Emir Wad en Nejumi were attacked by Grenfell with two brigades of Egyptian infantry, a regiment of British cavalry and a brigade of British infantry. In this action, which marked the turning-point in the tide of the Mahdist invasion, Kitchener was in command of the mounted troops and skilfully lured the Dervish force to destruction with the death of their leader. Kitchener was later appointed Sirdar of the Egyptian Army and, with the Dervishes far away in the south and peace reigning in Egypt, began to prepare his forces for an attempt to re-occupy the Sudan.

16
The Warriors of the Mahdi in the Sudan, 1883–5

Most typical of all Victorian campaigns was that in the Sudan when sun-helmeted British County regiments and straw-hatted Naval landing parties tried unsuccessfully to snatch Gordon from beleaguered Khartoum in 1884–5 and then avenged him thirteen years later. Where the '… sand of the desert was sodden red … with the blood of a square that broke …' and the Victorian soldier saw his foe as '… a pore benighted heathen … but a first-class fighting man …' His respect, freely given, was more than justified for, together with the Zulu (although never as organised) the generically named 'Fuzzy-Wuzzies' in appearance and fighting ability were among the fiercest natural warriors in the world. Their area was the Eastern Sudan, an arid scrub desert stretching 1,400 miles from the southern frontiers of Egypt to Uganda and the Congo (Zaire), where from 1880 to 1884 the nomadic tribes had been united by Mohammed Ahmed ibn Al-Sayid Abdullah, the self-styled Mahdi, whose gapped front teeth were a Sudanese luck-symbol – the Guided One of the Prophet – preaching Holy War to establish the Islamic faith across the whole of Northern Africa.

Although the Arabic name for the Sudan means 'Land of the Blacks', in colour the 600 tribes and 56 main tribal groups ranged from very black to light brown, divided into several major peoples – Beja in the area round Suakim, the Ababdeha in the north, the Bisharin south of Wadi Halfa and north of Debba, the Kababish, the Hassaniyeh and the Shaguyeh near Khartoum. South of Khartoum was the homeland of the Baggara people and near Abu Hamed the Amarca were the major tribe. Each was sub-divided, thus the Hadendowah were part of the Beja and the Taaisha were a division of the Baggara – then there were Beja–Hadendowah; Baggara–Taaisha; Ja'a-lyin; Danaqla; Batahin; Berberin; Barabra; Allanga; Duguaim; Kenana; Awadiyeh; Hamr-Kordofan; Darfureh; Monassir; Sowarab; Hau-hau-hin; Robatab; Base and Shukreeyah. The Mahdi's recruiting ground was the entire male population of the Sudan.

Numbers rapidly increased with an escalating series of victories over Egyptian forces sent to quell them, achieved by hurling themselves on the enemy when least expecting attack. Each triumph brought recruits from the defeated force with their arms and ammunition. Hauls from the annihilated Hicks Pasha and Baker expeditions included Krupp field-pieces, mountain guns, Nordenfelt machine-guns, and thousands of breech-loading Remington and Martini-Henry rifles.

By 1884 the Mahdi could call on thousands of horse and foot, a swelling horde of loyal fanatics clad in *jibbah*s, rough robes with vari-coloured patches symbolising virtuous poverty; this collection of regional armies became generally known as Dervishes, although to the Mahdi and his followers they were always the *ansar*, an Arabic word meaning helper or follower. The Mahdist army was centred first on Kordofan, then Khartoum or Omdurman, organised around the flags of his three main Khalifas; these 'flags' (*rayya*s) were semi-permanent forces augmented by tribal levies, divided into separate commands in different provinces. The Khalifa Abdallahi recruited the Baggara Arabs and other tribes from the West around the Black Flag (*al-rayya al-zarqa'*). The Khalifa al-Sharif's Red Flag (*al-rayya al-Hamra'*) was formed of warriors from the riverine peoples north of Khartoum, including Ja'aliyin and the Mahdi's own Danaqla. The Green Flag (*al-rayya al-Khadra'*) of the Khalifa Ali wad Hilu was drawn from the Dighaym, Kianan and al-Lahiwiyin Arabs of the Gezira region between the Blue and White Niles. Wherever the main army gathered, warriors were attached to one of these three flags, under their own *amir*s. The internal organisation of the various flags had groups of about twenty men under a *muggadam*; each force of 100 men under a *ra's mi'a*, grouped into several hundreds under the flag of an *amir*, organised around one of the major flags. The basic tactical unit was the *rub*, numerically flexible and ranging from several hundred men to a few thousand, but usually 800–1,200; the *rub* was sub-divided into an administrative and three combat units – spearmen, riflemen and cavalry, usually Baggara.

In 1883 a force of riflemen was formed of black Africans from the south and west who had been in the Egyptian army, or served in private armies of ivory- and slave-traders; known as the *jihadiyya,* it was developed and commanded by Hamdan Abu Anja. Armed with Remington rifles, it was a semi-autonomous group with different sections assigned to each flag and province. In 1892 the *jihadiyya* was superseded as the main rifle-force by the *mulazimiyya*, recruited from former *jihadiyya*, Western Arabs and recruits from the Nubian Mountains and the south; numbering about 10–12,000 and mostly armed with breech-loading rifles. From that year the main army was organised round the *mulazimiyya* and the Black Flag.

Below: Bisharin tribesmen fighting Egyptian troops near Suakim.

The outward and visible sign of adherence to the *mahdiyya* was the short, rough-cloth patched *jibbah*, reaching to the knees and well short of the wrists; irregularly patched as a necessity, later the vari-coloured patches became ordered and meaningful. In the early days, the Mahdi decreed that the *ansar* should wear this crude garment of the poor and lowly, with white trousers (*siraval*), sandals (*sayidan*), straw girdle (*karaba*), skull-cap (*taggia*), turban (*imma*) wrapped around the skull-cap with a tail (*aziba*) hanging free behind the left ear, a style as important a badge of Mahdism as the *jibbah*; and beads (*sibba*). The *jibbah* was white or greyish-white and patched in symmetrical designs with rectangular pieces of coloured cloth, two or three in front, one on each sleeve, and one on each side of the skirt; sometimes there were coloured rectangles under each arm, and collars were bordered by a triangular patch. The most common colours for patches were – black, dark and medium blue, various shades of red, blue, black or yellow. Manufactured in Omdurman, the *jibbah* was often issued to warriors at the start of a campaign, but it is unlikely that units were uniformly dressed with the same type. *Amir*s dressed much the same as the ordinary warrior, although their *jibbah* was sometimes more ornate and the patches were usually ornamentally embroidered and the 'club'-shaped breast pocket was similarly decorated. *Amir*s were always mounted, usually on fine Arab horses. Their saddles had high cantles and pommels, bridles were decorated with brass studs and coloured horse hair; the horse's face and rump were often coloured with fly-fringing. Subordinate officers wore a less ornate *jibbah,* but it could be distinguished from those of their men. Mahmud, Osman Digna and the Khalifa Sharif invariably wore a simple *jibbah*, and at Omdurman the Khalifa Abdullah is reported as wearing a blue-patched *jibbah* with a blue waistband, and riding a donkey under a parasol.

The usual *ansar* head-dress was a white turban wrapped around a white or solid-coloured skull-cap; some wore the skull-cap only, or went bareheaded. The Beja, Bisharin and some Baggara wore their hair long, frizzed and stiffened to stand-out as much as eight inches from the side of the head, then brushed to pile-up with a long wooden skewer through the top part. Other groups shaved the head except for a long tuft from the centre of the crown covered by a small straw-plaited or cotton skull-cap, sometimes covered with a cotton *pugaree*, the loose end wound under the chin and around the neck. Beja 'Fuzzy-Wuzzies' and Bisharin wore ankle-length white cotton trousers, or loincloths worn 'dhoti-fashion' around the waist, with a loose cotton scarf over the shoulders tucked into the waistband.

Exotic illustrations show Dervish cavalry wearing elaborate chainmail; but this was not worn in battle and perhaps the only unit thus dressed were the 200 Baggara of the Khalifa's body-guard, who were said to wear chain-mail and greaves, red sashes, and red turbans wound round iron helmets and under the chin; their horses wore brass headguards.

Each *amir*'s command was based on his flag, containing lesser amirs and leaders who also had their personal standards. Generally about 4 feet by 4 feet; black, blue, green or red, or a white background with coloured borders and letters, they bore passages from the Koran in Arabic on one side only. Staffs were decorated with brass balls, fist-topped globes or crescents, and horse-tails; the Khalifa's famous black flag was attached to a dark-red leather-covered staff, seventeen feet long.

Above: Bisharin or Baggara warriors.

Most Dervish warriors carried the 10-foot-long broad-bladed thrusting spear, plus short throwing spears, and the long straight double-edged razor-sharp sword with simple metal cross hilt; the red leather scabbard, worn under the armpit close to the body, was attached by metal rings and croc-odile-skin binding to a sling worn over the left shoulder. A short dagger in a red leather sheath was strapped to the upper arm under the *jibbah*; Beja and Bisharin tribesmen carried wicked knives with hooked blades broadening towards the tip. Shields were usually elliptical or round, with a raised conical

boss, made from rhinoceros, crocodile or elephant hide and reputed to deflect a bullet; they were seldom carried, except by the Beja. Firearms were restricted to the Jihadiyya and the Mulazamiyya, trained rifle-bearing infantry, who initially had captured Remington breech-loading rifles or percussion muzzle-loading muskets, but by the time of the Dongola Cam-paign all had either the Remington, Martini-Henry, Italian bolt-action mag-azine rifle, or the Belgian Alboni. Some of the Mulazamiyya carried flintlock pistols, and *amirs* occasionally had revolvers; riflemen did not carry any edged weapons except when short of ammunition, as they were in 1898 in Equatoria. Their musketry was reason-able although accuracy was impaired by a tribal habit of shortening the bar-rels of captured rifles, and they tended to fire high; after the war with Abyssinia, musketry standards deteri-orated as a result of heavy casualties, lack of ammunition and wear-and-tear of firearms. Riflemen wore no special uniform, having around the waist or shoulders one or two locally made bandoliers decorated with strips of coloured leather; those with muzzle-loading muskets carried cartridge-boxes and powder-horns.

The Mahdist army had an impres-sive number of cannon, some quite modern served by four chiefs and 152 Egyptian-trained artillerymen; but apart from reasonably effective fire from forts along the Nile against river-steamers in 1885 and 1896–7, little use was made of them. At the time of Omdurman they were known to have, either in the arsenal, in mud forts along the river, or mounted in captured river-boats, 63 guns: 35 brass mountain guns (howitzers); eight Krupp field-pieces; twelve assorted muzzle-loaders including a Remington (possibly a machine-gun); and a 'French' gun, plus six multi-barrelled Nordenfelt machine-guns. At the Battle of Omdurman in 1898, there were nineteen guns present: thirteen mountain guns; one Krupp; the Remington gun, and three Nordenfelts. Only five of them were actually known to have fired (from a hill overlooking the battlefield). A war correspondent noted their performance: 'more than forty rounds were fired from these Dervish field guns, but the shells did little, if any, damage as, although the fuses were beautifully timed and the projectiles burst at an excellent height above the ground, the range was too long and they all fell short. Moreover, after the fight some fragments of these shells were picked up and found to be made of very thin brass casing; so that the damage they could have inflicted, even had they reached our lines, must have been inconsiderable.' They fell short because locally-made shells had only a 500 yards' range – captured shells (in very short supply) could reach 2,500 yards – with few facilities for ammunition manufacture and local saltpetre bad, they could only make shells of light copper, with little shrapnel effect.

Three river-steamers had been acquired by the *ansar*: two of them, *Ismailia* and *al-Safia*, left behind by the Egyptian troops, had each been armed with a mountain gun. The other, *Bordein*, was one of the boats sent by Gordon to meet the Camel Corps at Mehtemma. Scuttled when the British retreated, she was raised and refitted by the Mahdists, but remained unarmed.

Their encounters taught the British at first hand what it was like to come up against the fanatically brave and ferocious ansar, from the moment a few flags appeared over a crest, then solid masses of tribesmen came into view, the bushes became alive with riflemen who swarmed unseen through the scrub, revealed only by little smoke puffs rising above the mimosa trees. The muffled roar of a vast crowd hung on the still, hot air, chanting '*La Illah illa'llah wa Muhammad rasul Allah*', backed by the incessant beating of drums. Contemporary accounts tell how disconcerting this could be – '... they had a knack of making their drums sound as if they were many miles away and the next moment they rose from the grass a few feet away from you ...'; a black cloud moving so rapidly forward that it astonished the British soldiers. Seemingly well-drilled, they manoeuvred in large phalanxes, each headed by a superbly mounted

Below: Gordon Relief Expedition, 1884. During a desert fight an Ansar warrior, probably Beja, penetrates the square.

and well-attended *amir*; jogging forward and increasing momentum in time with drum-beats, keeping-up with the galloping horses of their excited *amir*s, who stood in the stirrups and yelled encouragement.

Their tactics were based on surprise and shock, with riflemen screening sword- and spear-armed warriors, softening-up the enemy with their rapid fire; concealed in the scrub and making use of cover to get close before launching an attack, they came forward very fast in wedge-formation that inevitably widened the breach once the point had penetrated enemy ranks. Requiring neither drilling nor organisation, the wedge is a natural formation arising simply from the bravest warriors rushing to the front. At Abu Klea, masses of Dervishes rushed silently down on the left-front corner of the square, the ground quivering under the furious drumming of bare feet; they fell in waves as volleys crashed into them without stopping their charge. Trying to halt the onrushing Dervishes, soldiers sliced-off the heads of bullets, but even the huge wounds caused by these expanding missiles did not stop the courageous tribesmen. They hit the square with a spine-shaking impact, forcing the left face back on to the rear of the square's front face; once within, the avalanche was broken by frightened camels forming a living traverse and the centre became a maelstrom of desperate conflict, with camels, horses, uniformed soldiers and naked tribesmen welded together in a hacking, slashing, surging mass. The rear rank, forced up on to a steep little ridge within the square, were able to fire over the heads of front-rank men, into the heaving confusion of camels and Dervishes, until they began wavering. Then slowly and reluctantly, they turned away and walked off sullenly into the scrub, leaving the surrounding ground white with the *jibbahs* of the great heaps of dead behind them. Following up, there was the ever-present danger of wounded tribesmen lying in the scrub feigning death, shooting or slashing at all who came within reach.

Frantic firing soon caused dense clouds of smoke to hang on the still air, blending with dust to conceal the Dervishes and allow them to approach unseen, bursting like spectres from the haze, flourishing broad-bladed spears and cross-hilted swords, or creeping and crawling beneath the muzzles of rifles and guns, to erupt suddenly like malevolent jack-in-the-boxes, hacking and slashing with five-feet long swords, razor-sharp and capable of lopping off a man's arm or slicing off the top of his skull.

Cavalry always had a hard time against them as the Dervishes flung themselves to the ground and tried to hamstring passing horses with sickle-bladed knives; lancers thrust until the lances broke or could not be withdrawn from a body, then slashed with the sabre, but found it impossible to reach crouching or lying men. Later, General Stewart ordered the Hussars to convert Arab spears to lances by weighting the heads with rolls of sheet iron. Dervishes did not break under the shock of a cavalry charge – as undisciplined savages were supposed to do – instead they attacked horses with rifle butts, swung long heavy swords at mounts and riders, and hacked at horses legs with broad-bladed spears.

By April 1885, after horrendous casualties, most of the tribes had deserted Osman Digna and this part of the campaign was practically at an end. In January 1885, Earle's River Column struggled on until recalled, but Earle himself was killed; Wolseley arrived at Suakim, announced the campaign was to end, and in June 1885 returned to England. The Mahdi died of typhus, and was succeeded by the Khalifa Abdullahi.

17
The Formation of Native Regiments in Egypt and the Sudan from 1884

Shortly after Lord Wolseley's force destroyed the Egyptian Army at Tel-el-Kebir on 13 September 1882, the Khedive Tewfik announced '*l'Arm e egyptienne est dissoute*'. Subsequently, despite the view in some quarters of the British occupying force that a new Egyptian Army would be useless and a breeding-ground for further rebellion, Lord Dufferin decreed that a new army should be formed to keep internal order and protect the frontiers. Consisting mainly of Egyptians, its total strength would be about 6,000, and its officers and drill-sergeants would all be British. Led by Sir Evelyn Wood and later Sir Francis Grenfell, these dedicated men gradually grafted pride and a sense of purpose on to a motley force until a trained and disciplined army became a reality.

Prior to this, conditions in the old Egyptian army had been so bad – particularly for the men in the ranks – that under the new regime a fairly rapid and spectacular improvement was inevitable. Despite the widespread contempt for Arabi's soldiers among the British and Indian Army officers who had fought against them, the sturdy *fellahin* had many promising military aspects that could be built upon; regular pay and medical services greatly helped the enterprise, both morally and physically.

Right: The 11th Sudanese Infantry in action at Akasheh during the advance to Dongola

Left: An Egyptian cavalry patrol in trouble.

Recalling that the Sudanese regiments had been the only units of Arabi's army that had shown any fighting spirit during the 1882 campaign, British officers could not conceal their preference for the 'black' troops as they called them, and in May 1884 at Suakim, the first Sudanese battalion was recruited and mustered-in. Most of the men who enlisted were deserters from the Mahdi's army, Dinkas, Shilluks, Gallas and Dervishes who had been taken prisoner at El Teb and Tamai. In March 1885 General Sir Francis Grenfell became Sirdar, carrying on the good work of his predecessor, creating four more Sudanese battalions while generally strengthening and raising the standards of equip-

ment of the army. Over the years, the Sudanese battalions of the Egyptian army steadily enhanced their reputation; for example, the XIIth Sudanese Regiment became renowned for a bravery under fire that was second to none, and the Xth Regiment was adopted by the Lincolnshire Regiment (themselves the 10th of Foot) as an 'honorary Black Battalion'.

Initially it had not been contemplated that the new army would be used outside Egypt's borders, but this concept had to be changed following Hick's defeat in 1883 plus other sweeping Mahdist successes. Subsequently, Grenfell formed a force consisting of equal numbers of Egyptian and British troops, known as the Fron-

Left: An Egyptian artillery battery, with mixed camel/mule transport.

tier Field Force, which successfully defended the new frontier at Wadi Halfa for nearly a decade. It was a period when Grenfell had the satisfaction of leading his untried army against the Mahdists, to gain some notable victories, beginning with their baptism of fire at Toski in 1889, when an invading army was routed and their leader, Wad en Nejumi, was killed. This defeat forcibly brought home to the Mahdists the realisation that easy victories were no longer possible against what had become a very formidable army. The Egyptian Army, though having inferior equipment, and operating at comparatively low cost, had a consistent record of success in these campaigns, the enemy being worn down by sheer patience, pluck and a business-like approach.

Steadily increasing in size from the initial 6,000 men, by 1890 the Army strength was about 12,000 (including cavalry and artillery) through the raising of five Sudanese and eight 'fellahin' battalions. When Lord Kitchener became Sirdar, he continued the build-up by raising a sixth Sudanese battalion in 1896 and four more 'fellahin' battalions in the following year. Thus, when the Dongola Campaign began in 1896, the total muster-roll of Regular troops was eighteen battalions of infantry; ten squadrons of cavalry; a camel corps of eight companies; five batteries of artillery, plus the usual quota of engineers, medical staff, transport and other departmental troops. The new Egyptian Army taken by Kitchener to Khartoum was a very different force from the defeated army dissolved by British decree fourteen years earlier.

There was never any difficulty in raising recruits, the *fellahin* being attracted by the pay and general conditions of service while, after each victory, the more suitable prisoners and deserters were enlisted, to their great content, in one or other of the Sudanese battalions. After Omdurman in 1898, prisoners from the Khalifa's army were recruited *en bloc*, given a token uniform and a few days' drilling, and the warriors who had fought so energetically and gallantly against Kitchener's army now became part of it.

The normal strength of a battalion of infantry was 759 officers and men, divided into six companies, 100–120 strong; with band and bearer-parties, a battalion could field from 650 to 750 men armed with the Martini-Henry rifle. Their uniform was a brown jersey, sand-coloured trousers, with dark-blue putties; a fez-like cap (*tarboosh*) with a neck-cover for the Egyptian soldiers. The Sudanese (who needed no such protection) wore plaited-straw around the *tarboosh*, which also bore a badge whose colour varied according to the battalion. The strength of a cavalry squadron was about 100, with a British squadron-leader each; cavalrymen were always Egyptians; the front rank of each squadron carried a lance as well as a sabre and a Martini carbine; horses were stout, hardy beasts of about 13 hands, capable of very hard work. The two batteries of field-artillery were armed with the Maxim–Nordenfelt quick-firing 9-pounder gun, or 18-pounders with a double shell; both able to be drawn by two mules. The horse-battery was armed with Krupp 12- or 6-pounders. All the gunners were Egyptian, battery commanders were British. The camel-corps was about 800 strong, half Egyptian, half Sudanese, with five white officers; they used the mounted-infantry saddle, sitting astride, and carried the Martini-Henry rifle with bayonet.

Each infantry battalion had a British NCO instructor, responsible for teaching shooting, drill, etc. Technically subordinate to all native officers, these men's position was ambiguous. The normal number of white officers was three to an Egyptian battalion and four to a Sudanese, being increased to four and five respectively for the Dongola

Below: The Camel Corps on the way to Wadi Halfa.

Campaign of 1896–8; the 1st to 4th and 15th to 18th '*fellahin*' battalions had British officers, the 5th to 8th battalions, native officers, largely of Turkish, Circassian or Albanian origin although native Egyptians had furnished the army with some conspicuously useful officers. No British regimental officer took lower rank then major (*Bimbashi*); the lieutenant-colonel (*Kaimakam*) commanding a battalion was usually a Major or Captain in the British Army.

In addition to having 8,200 British troops at Omdurman in 1898, Kitchener's force included 17,600 Egyptian and Sudanese Regulars, formed as follows: nine squadrons of cavalry; one battery of Horse Artillery; four field batteries; ten Maxim guns; eight Camel Corps companies and the following infantry: 1st Brigade (2nd Egyptian Battalion, 9th, 10th and 11th Sudanese Battalions); 2nd Brigade (8th Egyptian Battalion, 12th, 13th and 14th Sudanese Battalions); 3rd Brigade (3rd, 4th, 7th and 15th Egyptian Battalions); 4th Brigade (1st, 5th, 17th and 18th Egyptian Battalions).

They served him well – the valour of the men of the 1st Brigade (MacDonald's) and their confidence in their resourceful commander, did much to save the day.

After the re-conquest of the Sudan, the Egyptian Army was reduced, and by the end of Lord Cromer's time in Egypt, in 1907, the strength of the army was 16,000 with 11,000 in reserve.

Left: The British Commanding officer of a Sudanese battalion watches his men embark at Shellal during the advance to Dongola.

18
Chronology of the Dongola–Omdurman Campaign, 1896–8

1885, 26 January: Fall of Khartoum; Gordon Killed; Mahdists take Kassala and Sennar

31 December: Battle of Ginnis

1887: Mahdist War with Abyssinia begins

1888, 20 December: Grenfell defeats Osman Digna at Gemaizeh and ends siege of Suakim

1889: Famine throughout the year

July: Mahdist Invasion of Egypt

3 August: Mahdists defeated at Battle of Toski

1891, 19 February: Egyptian Forces defeat Mahdists at Tokar; revolt against Khalifa crushed

1892, February: Grenfell resigns as Sirdar; **March:** Kitchener appointed Sirdar

1893, November: Italians defeat Mahdist force under Ahmad wad-Ali at Agordat

1894, July: Italians capture Kassala

1895: Slatin Pasha escapes from Khalifa

1896, 1 March: Abyssinians defeat Italians at Adowa

15: Hunter occupies Akasha

7 June: Battle of Firket

September: River bombardment of Hafir

23: Anglo/Egyptian Army enters Dongola

1897, 1 January: First sleepers laid for railway from Wadi Halfa to Abu Hamed

June: Khalifa sends Mahmud and Army of the West to Metemmeh

7 August: Hunter's Force storm Abu Hamed

21: Mahdists abandon Berber, after garrison mutiny

31: Kitchener occupies Berber

31 October: Railway reaches Abu Hamed

25 December: Kassala handed over to Egyptian Army by Italians

31: Sirdar asks for British reinforcements

1898, 26 February: British brigade leaves Abu Dis for front

3 March: Reaches Dibeika, beyond Berber

15: Sirdar leaves Berber

16: Concentration at Kenu

20: Army moves up the Atbara

21: First contact with Dervish cavalry

27: Shendi raided and destroyed

30: General Hunter reconnoitres Mahmud's *zareba*

4 April: Second reconnaissance; cavalry action before Mahmud's *zareba*

8: Battle of the Atbara

11: Sirdar's triumphal entry into Berber

18: Railhead reaches Abeidieh; construction of gunboats begun

Mid-June: Railhead reaches Fort Atbara

Early July: Lewis's Brigade leaves Atbara for south

3–17 August: 2nd British Brigade arrives at Atbara

13: Sirdar leaves Atbara for front
18: Last troops leave Atbara
28: Final concentration at Gebel Royan
29: March from Gebel Royan to Wadi Abid (eight miles)
30: March from Sayal to Wadi Suetne (ten miles)
31: Kerreri reconnoitred and shelled; march from Wadi Suetne to Agaiga (six miles)

1 September: Omdurman reconnoitred and forts silenced
2: Battle of Omdurman and capture of Khartoum
4: Funeral of Gordon
9: Sirdar leaves for Fashoda
22: Battle of Gedaref
24: Sirdar returns from Fashoda

Below: Top, General Archibald Hunter and Major-General Rundle. Centre, Slatin Pasha. Bottom, General Burn-Murdoch and Colonel Wingate.

19
Kitchener's Dongola–Omdurman Campaign, 1896–8

In the years that followed Gordon's death at Khartoum, the British public demanded insistently that he be avenged. This, together with the increasing activity of the French, Belgians and Italians in Africa, finally prompted the British Government in March 1896 to instruct General Kitchener to undertake a campaign of reconquest in Egypt. The campaign opened on 16 March 1896 when several Egyptian battalions were hurried up the Nile by rail and in the river-steamers of Messrs. Thomas Cook and Sons, to garrison Akasha and the various Posts between there and Wadi Halfa which was to be garrisoned by the North Staffords. A fortified camp was made at Akasha to cover the railway construction, and here supplies for a further advance were to be accumulated by camel convoys following the river route while reinforcements and supplies came up the Nile from Egypt.

Kitchener had solved the problem of supply for his Dongola Expeditionary Force by taking advantage of river transport supplemented by camels and by extending the railway as he progressed. By these means he intended to concentrate his striking force and drive the enemy from Firket. Next, when the Nile rose, the reserve troops and supplies accumulated at Firket would be carried in sailing-boats

Right: The transportation of Egyptian troops up the Nile at the start of the Dongola Campaign in 1896. Officers travelled in the centre stern-wheeler, the troops in barges lashed to each side of the steamer.

Left: Hauling the gunboat *El Teb* up the Second Cataract, through the 'Big Gate'.

Below: Lewis's 1st Brigade, during the Battle of Firket, clears the river bank, storming the outworks of the Jahlin Camp.

BATTLE OF FIRKET
JUNE 7 1896

Above: Charge of the Egyptian cavalry at the Battle of Firket.

up to Dongola in the wake of the army, while the shallow-draught gun-boats would assist and guard the river traffic and take part in the fighting.

During the fourteen years that had elapsed since the British evacuation of the Sudan, an Egyptian army had been created that was capable of fighting alongside their British comrades and holding their own against the hitherto dreaded Dervishes. Many of the soldiers in these battalions had originally fought against the British because, after each victory, the best of the prisoners and deserters were enlisted in Egyptian battalions where British sergeant-instructors taught them to drill and shoot.

News of the rapid movement of the Egyptian Army, and of reinforcements on their way from Suakim, reached the Khalifa at Omdurman and, under the Emir Hammuda, the Dervishes began to mass in great force at Firket and other places to the south. In char-

acter, they had not altered appreciably since the battles of the early 1880s, retaining all their old dash and fire although their spears and Remington rifles were no match for the hard-hitting Martini-Henry rifles of the new Egyptian Army.

Throughout May 1896 Kitchener consolidated his position at Akasha, bringing up more troops and improving his communications so that by the end of the month the railway line stretched 64 miles from Wadi Halfa and was only 25 miles from Akasha. Then Kitchener sent a force of Egyptian and Sudanese soldiers with British Maxim-gun teams by both the river and desert routes to pounce upon Hammuda and his 3,000 tribesmen at Firket, sixteen miles upstream from Akasha. With secrecy, silence and perfect timing, the force surprised the Dervishes at 5 a.m. on 7 June 1896 and by 7.30 a.m., after very hard fighting, had beaten them, killing or wounding more than 1,000 men, and taking more than 500 prisoners.

During the three months that followed this decisive victory, the advance was delayed by storms, floods and cholera. Nevertheless, despite the dreadful weather, advance parties of troops penetrated far up the river, but when Lewis's Egyptian Brigade was caught in a dust-storm, 1,700 men of 3,000 collapsed and several died overcome by heat, thirst and exhaustion.

Kitchener had had a gunboat, the *Zafir,* brought up in sections and reassembled at Kosha. After incredible difficulties in putting it together again, its boiler burst immediately after launching and it was out of action for some months.

Reinforced by the arrival of the North Staffords, the Dongola Expeditionary Force of nearly 15,000 men advanced southwards in brigade formations along the desert route and river-bank, some units making the journey in river steamers protected by gunboats. On 18 September the Emir of Dongola transferred his troops across the Nile to an entrenched position on the left bank at Hafir, forcing Kitchener to open the way to Dongola solely with his gunboats and artillery, the infantry being unable to cross the broad and swift-flowing Nile that ran between the opposing forces. Watched by battalions of Egyptian infantry sitting on the hot sand, the three-hour action took place on the following day when the gunboats ran the gauntlet of the hostile batteries and steamed onwards to reach Dongola before sunset. The Emir evacuated Hafir and the Egyptian infantry crossed the Nile in boats abandoned by the Dervishes. Kitchener received the surrender of Dongola on the evening of the 24th. During the arduous six months' campaign, the Egyptian Army had lost only 47 soldiers killed, 122 wounded and about 350 missing.

To maintain the successful momentum of the Dongola Expedition, Kitchener decided to build a railway from Wadi Halfa to Abu Hamed, across the uncharted and waterless Nubian Desert. The first sleepers were laid on 1 January 1897, and by 15 July the railway had been pushed almost halfway across the desert towards Abu Hamed, when the work was held up while a force was sent to throw the enemy out of that place.

Commanded by Major-General Archibald Hunter with Lieutenant-Colonel Hector MacDonald, a flying column consisting of an Egyptian and Sudanese infantry brigade, a mule

Below: The gun-boat *Zaffir* reconnoitring Osman Digna's position at Shendy.

battery of six Krupp 12-pounders guns, four machine-guns, a few cavalry and 1,300 camels, toiled painfully through a miserable wilderness of rock and ankle-deep white sand to cover 118 miles in 7½ days at the hottest time of the year. Completely surprising the Dervishes, the Sudanese infantry rushed the trenches with the bayonet and achieved a quick victory. Hunter had the Arab dead thrown into the river so that, two days later, Kitchener at Merowe, seeing a procession of Arab corpses floating downstream, knew that a battle had been won.

Disheartened and perturbed by the sudden advance, the enemy evacuated Berber, strategically the most vital point between Wadi Halfa and Omdurman, which was occupied by Kitchener on 31 August. Holding a long line, vulnerable to attack at many points, with a small force at Berber and in front of him a large army of warlike Dervishes, Kitchener realised that the time had come to ask for reinforcements of British troops. On 2 January the 1st Battalion Royal Warwickshire Regiment at Alexandria and the 1st Battalions of the Lincolnshire Regiment and the Cameron Highlanders at Cairo proceeded immediately to Wadi Halfa. The 1st Battalion Seaforth Highlanders at Malta and the 5th Battalion Northumberland Fusiliers at Gibraltar were also brought to Egypt. These British infantry regiments formed a brigade under Colonel William Gatacre.

At the end of January 1898, the general situation was that the Egyptian Army, composed of three infantry brigades, eight squadrons of cavalry and four batteries of artillery, held various Posts along the Nile from Fort Atbara to Abu Hamed, and the British brigade under Gatacre was in camp thirty miles south of Abu Hamed. The Suakim–Berber route had been opened and its oases were held by armed Posts. An Egyptian garrison defended Kassala, about 250 miles east of Khartoum, which the British had taken over from the Italians after their defeat at Adowa. Arrangements had been made with the Abyssinians to remain neutral. The main Dervish army, 40,000 strong, was with the Khalifa at Omdurman with a further 20,000 men under Mahmud and Osman Digna at Metemmeh.

In February, the Khalifa allowed Mahmud to cross the Nile; having done so, he found himself in an angle formed by the Nile and the Atbara from which

Below:
Colonel Hector A. MacDonald.

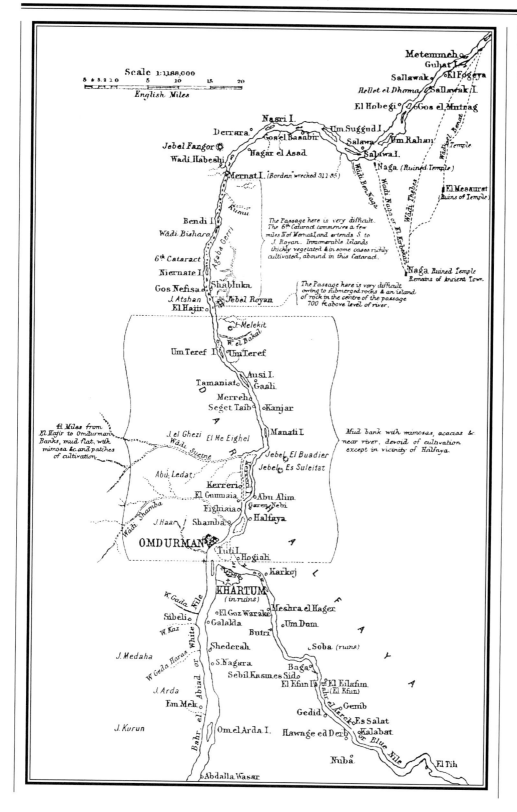

Left: The sector of the River Nile about Omdurman and Khartoum.

Above: The Sirdar's flotilla – the gunboats on the Nile.

At last Kitchener struck camp and moved upstream to assault the Dervish position with a force consisting of about 14,000 men with 24 guns and twelve machine-guns; it included the British Brigade; an Egyptian Division of three infantry brigades; eight squadrons of Egyptian cavalry; six companies of the Camel Corps and a Rocket Detachment together with two British and two Egyptian Maxim batteries. On 8 April, formed into four great brigade squares with the British leading, under the light of a bright moon the force trudged across the desert until 4 a.m. when they deployed into attack formation.

Advancing through the scattered bush and scrub, they reached open ground overlooking the shallow crater-like depression where less than half a mile away, lay Mahmud's stronghold. At 6.20 a.m. the first gun fired on the *zareba*, followed by a heavy cross-fire of shells and rockets that set trees, bushes and straw huts alight so that clouds of smoke rolled over the enemy's trenches while earth and stones flew in all directions. Prone in their deep trenches, the Dervishes showed no signs of life except once when hundreds of horsemen scrambled into the saddle and galloped out to the Egyptian left front where they were hotly engaged by the cavalry and machine-guns. At 7.40 a.m. the bombardment ceased and the General Advance was sounded. Then, with bands playing, pipes skirling and shouts of 'Remember Gordon!' the lines and columns of infantry bore down on the Dervish *zareba*. The British had the Cameron Highlanders in line along their entire front, then, in columns of their eight companies, the Lincolns on the right, the Seaforths in the centre and the Warwicks on the left, all halting to volley-fire by sections and moving off again at the sound of the bugle.

he could not retreat without giving battle. Short of supplies and his force dwindling through desertions, Mahmud and his 12,000 followers entrenched themselves on the right bank of the Atbara and awaited the attack. The British brigade moved up and bivouacked within ten miles of Atbara Fort. Unable to tempt the Dervishes from their entrenched position, and conscious that his army was nearly 1,400 miles from the sea and about 1,200 miles from its main base of supplies and had to be supplied along a sand banked river and along a single railway line which was also carrying the material for its own construction, Kitchener hesitated to attack. The delay caused considerable hardship to the troops who had only one blanket and no overcoat so that they suffered badly from the cold at night and the heat during the day. Also, poor food and inadequate sanitary conditions caused dysentery and enteric fever to make their appearance.

It had been reported that Mahmud's position was fronted by a dense and extremely prickly thorn hedge, but when the Cameron Highlanders came up to the position they found it was only a low barrier of dry, loose camel thorn that was easily pulled aside. Inside the zareba was a stockade and triple trench amid bush thick with palm stem, mimosa thorn and scrub grass, dotted with a honeycomb of holes and pits. When the infantry stormed into the *zareba* there was no sign of life, but suddenly out of the earth leapt dusty, black figures running and turning to shoot as they fell back before the advancing infantry. Leaving the ground behind them carpeted thickly with dead tribesmen, the Camerons, Seaforths and Lincolns deployed right

Right: Bird's eye view of the advance at the Battle of the Atbara.

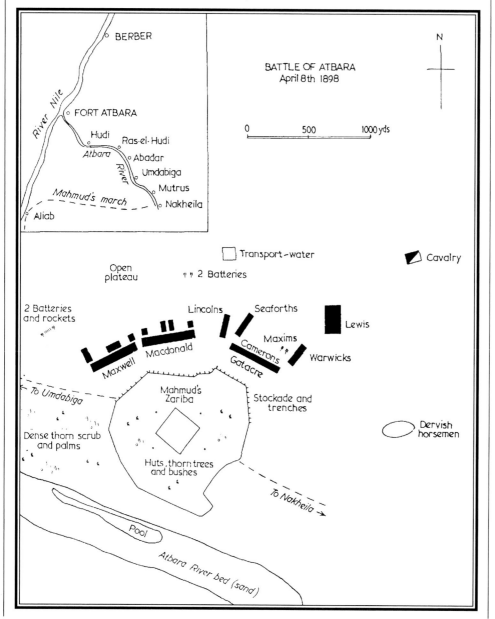

Right: The Battle of the Atbara – the final charge.

and left to sweep straight across the *zareba* to the rear entrenchment and beyond through thick undergrowth to the river. The troops thronged the river bank in double line and fired crashing volleys into the fleeing natives across the quarter-mile of dry sand bed until it was dotted with huddled black shapes. With some difficulty the troops were finally restrained from firing, then there was a sudden silence followed by a loud burst of cheering and the forty-minute battle was over.

The British Brigade lost 5 officers and 21 men killed and 99 officers and men wounded; the three Egyptian brigades lost 57 men killed and 386 wounded including ten British officers. The Dervish losses are unknown, but were estimated at 40 Emirs and 3,000 men killed and many captured including Mahmud himself, so that Osman Digna and only 4,000 of the 12,000 who had garrisoned the position managed to rejoin the Dervish army at Omdurman.

The victorious force marched northwards to go into summer quarters along the Nile. Here, during July and August, they were reinforced by a new British Brigade formed of the 1st Bn., Grenadier Guards from Gibraltar; the 1st Battalion Northumberland Fusiliers and the 2nd Battalion Lancashire Fusiliers from Cairo and the 2nd Battalion The Rifle Brigade from Malta while the 21st Lancers were sent up from Egypt, together with considerable artillery reinforcements. The force now totalled more than 22,000 men, with 44 guns and twenty Maxims plus three new gunboats which were put together immediately after the battle of Atbara.

On 24 August the army began to move southwards by successive divisions, preceded by the cavalry and the Camel Corps and marching on a 2-brigade front in a formation well adapted for repelling a sudden assault. On 31 August they came to a hilltop and looking down saw Omdurman, an extensive area of mud houses with the Mahdi's tomb rising amidst them. Before the town, noticeable at first only because of their banners, was a

Above: At the close of the fight in the zareba at the Battle of the Atbara.

solid wall of motionless warriors drawn up in five immense masses on a 3-mile front, eight or ten deep, totalling perhaps 40,000 men.

Expecting to be attacked, Kitchener ordered the searchlights of his gunboats to be turned on the enemy's camp throughout the night; his infantry lay down behind a low fence of thorn bushes in a shallow trench about a foot deep with a raised parapet in front, and the mounted troops withdrew inside the enclosure. As on the afternoon of the previous day, at daylight on 2 September, the gunboats and 5-inch howitzers bombarded Omdurman at more than 3,000 yards' range, throwing 50-pound shells that tore great holes in the dome of the Mahdi's tomb.

Now the Khalifa, unacquainted with battle since 1885, and, with the exception of Osman Digna, having only untried or undependable commanders, instead of awaiting attack in the hilly area around his capital of Omdurman, obligingly flung his *ansar* at Kitchener's well-defended *zareba* on the banks of the Nile. Said to be about 40,000 strong, it was formed of the Khalifa's Guard of about 1,000 men in two *rubs*, one with Remingtons, the other divided among Khashkhashkan, wearing red waistcoats over the *jibbah* and armed with percussion elephant-guns on tripods; Mushammaratiya, tall natives with long spears; and axe-armed Bultagia. The Mulazamiyya, under Uthman Shaykh al-Din, 10,000 riflemen in eighteen *rubs*, were subdivided into 8–10 standards each 100 strong. The Omdurman Garrison led by Ibrahim Khalil, 2,500 in 500 standards were divided into three main and three lesser *rubs*, half of them armed with rifles. Uthman Azraq's 'flag' of 8,000 men were under six *amirs*. Green Flag (Abdallah abu Siwar) numbered 2,500 in three tribal *rubs* under five *amirs*. Black Flag led by Amir

Yaqub, numbered 12,000 men in 51 standards, with less than a thousand firearms, and, finally, the 7,000 natives of Osman Digna. This savage and courageous army were described by Winston Churchill (who fought there) and others as – '... a might army, its huge banners flying, drums beating and spears flashing ... in the clear morning air the pageant was truly magnificent, a splendid panorama of 40,000 barbarians all moving forward to do battle with the largest army that Great Britain had placed in the field for forty years ...' An *Illustrated London News* correspondent mentions the sound of the Dervish Army as 'a loud continuous murmur of prayer chanting culminating with increased drum tempo in the whole line sweeping forward with a mighty roar..'

At daylight on 2 September, the cavalry and Camel Corps went out in a wide screen to reconnoitre, soon sending back messages that the entire Dervish army was advancing. At first a few flags appeared over the crest, then followed solid masses of spearmen and riflemen led by horsemen and the muffled roar of a vast multitude reached the ears of the waiting Anglo-Egyptian army as the Dervishes spread themselves in a gigantic semicircle round the front and left of the position. Ordered by Kitchener to draw the enemy across his front, the Egyptian cavalry and the Camel Corps with the Horse Artillery retired northwards towards the Karari Hills, and were followed by 20,000 Dervishes mustered under green flags. At 6.50 a.m. the artillery opened fire at 2,700 yards' range, next the gunboats on the southern flank opened up and the Grenadier Guards fired section volleys at 2,000 yards. As the Dervishes came within range, the Highlanders, the Lincolnshires and the Egyptian brigades took up the firing, standing in double

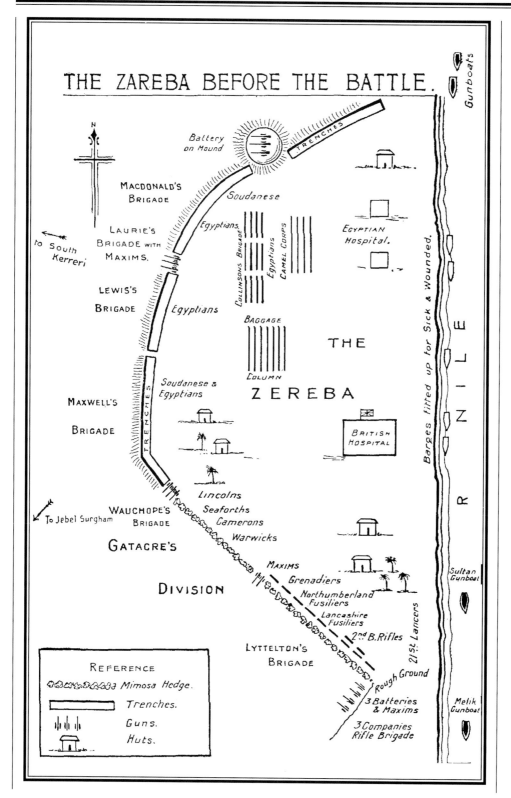

Left: A contemporary diagram showing the Sirdar's dispositions at the Battle of Omdurman.

Right: Inside the zareba at Omdurman – 6.30 a.m.

rank behind their low *zareba*, shooting as fast as they could load and squeeze trigger until the rifles got so hot that they had to be exchanged for others taken from the supports. As the guns bellowed, shrapnel whistled and Maxims growled savagely, the Dervishes advanced in a well-defined line, divided into masses of about 4,000 men covering the whole plain between the hills and the whole ridge from Jebel Surkab to the river. The never-ending hail of bullets and shells prevented a single Dervish from getting closer to the Anglo-Egyptian position than about 300 yards, and at 8 a.m. the survivors sullenly withdrew towards the west, leaving the ground white with

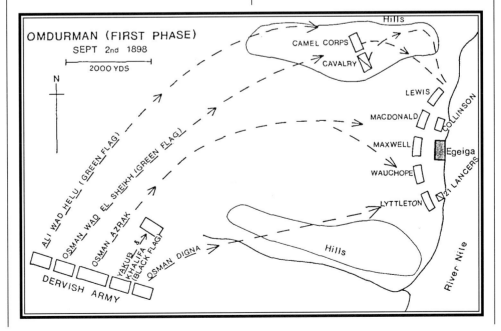

the *jibbah*s of more than 2,000 dead.

The cavalry and the Camel Corps had taken up a position on the Karari Hills, but, outflanked by vastly superior numbers of enemy, were in great difficulty. The Camel Corps particularly proving to be quite unable to contend with the mobile enemy in rocky ground. The Dervishes pressed the attack, capturing two guns and almost succeeding in isolating the Camel Corps, but at a critical moment a gun-

Left: The gunboat *Melik* saving the Camel Corps from destruction.

Below: A Royal Marine Artillery Sergeant supervises the fire from a gunboat upon hostiles on the river bank.

Right: A trooper of the 21st Lancers.

boat appeared from upstream and, assisted by the fire of the land artillery, drove the pursuers back with very heavy losses.

At 8.30 a.m. Kitchener sent the 21st Lancers forward to reconnoitre and clear the ground while the force broke up and expanded to march in echelon of brigades from the left to guard against an attack on the right flank or rear. It is possible that Kitchener was unaware that on his right front, hidden behind Jebel Surkab, lay the Army of the Black Flag, 17,000-strong under the Khalifa himself. Movement was slow as the 2nd British Brigade led the way along the river, the 1st British on their right rear, followed by the Egyptian brigades of Maxwell, Lewis and MacDonald, with Collinson supporting.

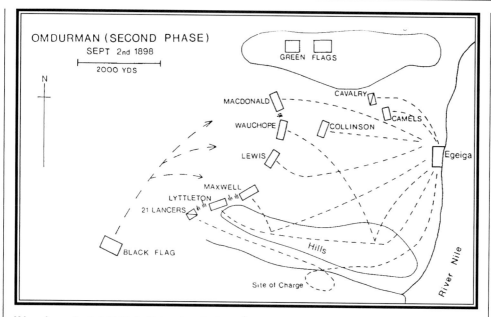

OMDURMAN (SECOND PHASE)
SEPT 2nd 1898
2000 YDS
N
GREEN FLAGS
MACDONALD
CAVALRY
WAUCHOPE
COLLINSON
CAMELS
LEWIS
Egeiga
MAXWELL
LYTTLETON
21 LANCERS
BLACK FLAG
Hills
River Nile
Site of Charge

Wauchope's 1st British Brigade tried to overtake Lyttleton's 2nd British Brigade with the result that Maxwell's 2nd Egyptian Brigade was outdistanced. Maxwell tried to close the widening gap between him and Wauchope, and Lewis hurried to reduce the interval between him and Maxwell, leaving MacDonald, having completed his move westwards towards the flank, nearly a mile from Lewis.

As Kitchener ordered Maxwell's Brigade to storm Jebel Surkab, with the 2nd British Brigade on his left, the Army of the Black Flag rushed out fiercely to attack MacDonald's and Lewis's Egyptian Brigades. Kitchener immediately sent the 1st British Brigade hurrying back to MacDonald's assistance so that, by these movements, the army now faced west with its right flank drawn back to the river. The Black Flag Army attacking MacDonald were taken in flank by the fire of Lewis's Brigade and also by Maxwell's Brigade which had captured the Jebel, causing them to waver and drift back. Suddenly, a howling storm of 12,000 unbroken and fearless warriors, the Green Flag Army, came

storming down from the Karari Hills on to MacDonald's right rear, forcing him to form his Egyptian Brigade into an arrow-head as Wauchope came up rapidly with his brigade, sending the Lincolns to the right and the remainder of the brigade to the left of Mac-Donald. Now began the fiercest fight of the day as the Khalifa brought up his own Black Banner warriors again to surge forward with the Green Flag Army.

This was a grave moment; if Mac-Donald went, Lewis on his left, with Collinson and the supporting Camel Corps and the cavalry who had returned from a charge, must all go too. The 2nd British and 2nd Egyptian Brigades, advancing by the left of Surkab Hill, were too far away to help. The Egyptian, Sudanese and British infantry poured volley after volley into the attacking tribesmen and then Mac-Donald and his Egyptian infantry drove the Army of the Green Flags back towards the hills and a charge by the Egyptian cavalry turned their retreat into a rout. Then, in an imposing array of artillery, cavalry and camels, the entire army advanced

Above: 'The 21st Lancers' charge – an exciting moment!' (The original caption to the picture when first published in the contemporary issue of *The Illustrated London News*.)

westwards, driving the Dervishes before them into the desert.

Immediately before all this had happened, the 21st Lancers with four squadrons in line, came upon a force of about 300 Dervishes on an apparently open plain and swung into the first charge of their history. Suddenly they came upon a yawning ravine packed with a solid mass of 3,000–4,000 Dervishes. Too late to check, the Lancers surged down the

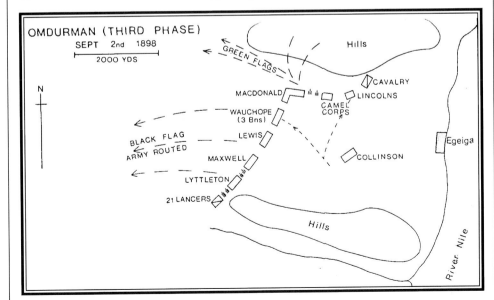

steep side of the ravine, their horses plunging and falling while Dervishes lay on the ground endeavouring to hamstring them. The cavalry went straight through and clear out the other side, leaving behind five officers, 65 men and 119 horses, to dismount and open fire with their carbines at short range before getting themselves clear.

At 11.30 a.m. the battle was over. The Dervish army had been wiped out, losing 11,000 killed, 16,000 wounded and 4,000 prisoners from their total of about 40,000 men. The Anglo-Egyptian Army, numbering perhaps 22,000 men, lost 48 killed and 382 wounded. The force marched on to meet very little resistance in the narrow evil-smelling streets of Omdurman. The Khalifa escaped and remained at large until November 1899 when a force of Native Infantry under Colonel Sir Reginald Wingate defeated the remaining Dervish Army and found the dead bodies of the Khalifa and his brothers on the battlefield.

Above: A corner of the battlefield; a standard bearer's death grip.

Left: British troops marching past the Mahdi's tomb.

Epilogue

Shifting the balance of power in Asia heavily in Britain's favour, Russia's defeat by Japan in 1905 brought the 'Great Game' to an enforced conclusion. However, it did not dramatically and suddenly transform the Pathans of the North-West Frontier into pacifists and, in the 1920s and 1930s the Frontier was a hotbed of trouble as Communist Russia sought every opportunity to sabotage British influence in Asia, particularly in Afghanistan, which seemed likely to resume its role of providing the terrain for a modern 'Great Game'. It was a time when the Frontier was the sole remaining area in the British Empire where young Britons could emulate the Kiplingesque feats of their forebears.

The break-up of the German East African empire in 1919 so extended Britain's colonial possessions that control of Egypt had to be maintained, that country being on the road to both Africa and India. Immediately prior to the Second World War, Hitler masterminded an abortive plot to throw the whole Frontier into a violent anti-British revolt that would pin down the greater part of the Anglo-Indian Army in India. In the event, the six years of that war marked a period of calm on the Frontier, the tribesmen serving overseas in British uniforms, coming back to their home ground to resume where they had left off.

During both wars, Egypt was neutral and occupied by a belligerent power – Britain – whose chief concern in 1914–18 had been to hold the Suez Canal against the Turks, and in 1939–45, when Egypt was much more territorially involved, to prevent occupation by German and Italian armies.

The Suez fiasco in 1956 marked the death-throes of British control over Egypt, but before then – on 31 March 1956 – the last British troops on Egyptian soil, the 2nd Battalion Grenadier Guards and 'D' Squadron The Life Guards, had embarked from Port Said.

Subsequently, the British soldier has had to face fervent nationalists in Malaya, Kenya, Cyprus, Aden and Northern Ireland, none of whom have come anywhere near achieving that high degree of respect accorded to the Dervish and the Pathan.

Reference Sources

Archer, Thomas. *The War in Egypt and the Soudan, 1886–7*

Atteridge, A. Hilliard. *The Wars of the 90s.* 1899

Bond, Brian. *Victorian Military Campaigns.* 1967

Burleigh, Bennett. *The Khartoum Campaign.* 1899

Callwell, Colonel C. E. *Small Wars: Their Principle and Practice.* 1895, 1976

Churchill, Winston. *The Story of the Malakand Field Force.* 1898

Elliott, Major-General J. G. *The Frontier, 1839–1947.* 1970

Farwell, Byron. *Queen Victoria's Little Wars.* 1973

Featherstone, Donald. *Colonial Small Wars.* 1973

– *Khartoum 1885.* 1993

– *Omdurman 1989.* 1995

– *Tel-el Kebir 1882.* 1993

– *The Life and Times of The Victorian Soldier.* in preparation

– *Victoria's Enemies.* 1989

– *Weapons and Equipment of the Victorian Soldier.* 1978

Field, Colonel C. *Britain's Sea Soldiers.* 1924

Graham, C. A. L. *The History of the Indian Mountain Artillery.* 1957

Grant, James. *Cassell's History of the War in the Soudan.* 1887

Leslie, N. B. *The Battle Honours of the British and Indian Armies, 1695–1914*

Manfield, Peter. *The British in Egypt.* 1871

Mason, Philip. *A Matter of Honour.* 1974

Maurice, John F. *Military History of the Campaign of 1882 in Egypt.* 1887

Miller, Charles. *Khyber.* 1977

Sandes, Lieutenant-Colonel E. W. C. *The Military Engineer in India.* 1933

– *The Royal Engineers in Egypt and the Sudan.* 1937

Steevens, G. W. *With Kitchener To Khartoum.* 1898

Swinson, Arthur. *North West Frontier: People And Events, 1839–1947.* 1967

Battles of the 19th Century: Described by Forbes, Archibald, Henty, G. A., Griffiths, Arthur, *et al.* 1902

The Illustrated London News, 1845–1901

Savage and Soldier Magazine (USA)

Soldiers of the Queen (Journal of the Victorian Military Society)

The British Empire (Part-Publication BBC/Time Life Books, 1972)

Frontier and Overseas Expeditions from India (Intelligence Branch, Army H.Q., India 1910)

Sudan Intelligence Reports, Egyptian Army (Cairo, 1896–9)

Index